# WELCOME TO YOUR JOURNAL.

The purpose of this journal is to help guide you through the coming year and help you to better understand the effects of the moon. The moon has an affect on everything and everyone, which is why it is so important to be aware of the effects and know how to handle them each month. Each moon phase is important, and we must understand them in order to harness the energy and use it to our advantage.

## THIS MOON JOURNAL INCLUDES:
- Details + Journal Prompts for each Moon Phase
- Moon Affirmations and Rituals
- Monthly + Yearly Reflection Questions
- Crystal Guidance, Self-Care Tips and More...

I hope this journal helps you to reach your highest potential this year through self-exploration, mindfulness and deep-thinking.

Please find our other books, journals and notebooks available on Amazon by searching for Mystic Tortoise or by visiting the link in the back of this journal.

Love and Light,
Mystic Tortoise

# MOON PHASES

## NEW MOON
*new beginnings*

## WAXING CRESCENT
*set intentions*

## FIRST QUARTER
*take action*

## WAXING GIBBOUS
*refine & nurture*

## FULL MOON
*harvest your intentions*

## WANING GIBBOUS
*introspection*

## LAST QUARTER
*release*

## WANING CRESCENT
*surrender*

# QUESTIONS FOR THE NEW YEAR

WHAT WOULD I BE MOST HAPPY ABOUT ACHIEVING THIS YEAR?

WHAT IS ONE THING I CAN DO TO REDUCE MY STRESS THIS YEAR?

WHAT DO I WANT TO LEARN MORE OF THIS YEAR?

HOW CAN I ADD 5 MINUTES OF PERSONAL TIME TO MY SCHEDULE EACH DAY THIS YEAR? HOW WILL I USE THIS TIME?

self care is

*self-love*
*self-worth*
*self-respect*

take care of yourself

# JANUARY 2022

1st WANING CRESCENT
2nd NEW MOON
3rd-8th WAXING CRESCENT
9th FIRST QUARTER
10th-16th WAXING GIBBOUS
17th FULL MOON
18th-24th WANING GIBBOUS
25th LAST QUARTER
26th-31st WANING CRESCENT

(EST USA Time Zone)

# WANING CRESCENT — JAN 1ST

The Waning Crescent Moon represents a period of surrender and a time for rest.

## IN SAGITTARIUS

## CRYSTALS FOR THIS MOON

Bloodstone - helps to embrace the transformation you have been through
Rainbow Fluorite - helps to balance emotions during this up and down period
Black Tourmaline - Grounds your spirit, deflects negative energies
Petalite - Brings peace and calm, supports working with Spirit and angel guides
Black Obsidian - Gently grounding and protective, strengthens your aura field

## MOON AFFIRMATION

I remain centered while my emotions change, and I release any emotions I have been repressing. I can remain balanced and take time to care for myself.

## MOON RITUAL

This moon marks the end of the healing cycle. Think of anything you need to do to complete this cycle before the next one begins. Be gentle to yourself and practice some self-care during this time. Do anything that relaxes you and helps you to feel calm and secure. Take a bath with your crystals surrounding you.

# WANING CRESCENT          JAN 1ˢᵀ

HOW CAN I IMPROVE MY SELF-CARE?




HOW AM I FEELING DURING THIS MOON PHASE?




WHAT DO I NEED TO DO FOR MYSELF?




IS THERE ANYTHING IN MY LIFE HOLDING ME BACK?
HOW CAN I LET GO?

# NEW MOON GUIDE  JAN 2ND

The Moon will be located on the same side of the Earth as the Sun which means you cannot see the moon from Earth.

## MOON IN CAPRICORN

The New Moon in Capricorn brings an increased awareness for your need of discipline and structure. This is a good time to work on your budget, being more responsible in certain areas of your life and setting good goals. Now is a time to focus on being stable and patient. This is the best time for planning, organizing, and checking in with yourself to make sure you are on the right path for reaching your goals that you have been setting. If you are a Capricorn, you will feel a stronger effect

## NEW MOON CRYSTALS

Charge your crystals in this new moon. Leave them out for two nights. You cannot see the moon at this time, but the cleansing is still powerful. Crystals that are powerful in the Capricorn New Moon are: Amethyst, Azurite, Merlinite, Malachite, Clear Quartz, Smoky Quartz, and Tangerine Quartz. Set your intentions for stability and remaining grounded and centered.

## NEW MOON RITUAL

Use sage to smudge your space for the ritual. Light a candle. Write down your intentions for the next month on a piece of paper. Meditate on your intentions. In a safe place, light the paper on fire to send your intentions into the universe. Then, take a few moments for yourself. Read a book, take a quiet walk, pray, meditate or rest. Take your crystals to bed with you tonight. You can feel the effects of the moon up to a week before and after it occurs.

# NEW MOON                                    JAN 2ND

The New Moon represents a fresh start and new beginnings.

GOALS FOR THIS MOON CYCLE:




HOW AM I FEELING DURING THIS MOON PHASE?




HOW CAN I EXPERIENCE MORE JOY AND PEACE?




WHAT IN MY LIFE NEEDS NOURISHMENT?

# WAXING CRESCENT  JAN 3RD-8TH

The Waxing Crescent Moon Phase represents setting intentions. This moon phase also represents positive changes in your emotional state.

3RD IN CAPRICORN
4TH-5TH IN AQUARIUS
6TH-7TH IN PISCES
8TH IN ARIES

## CRYSTALS FOR THIS MOON

Amethyst - brings inspiration, awakens insight and intuition
Citrine - stimulates the brain, promotes motivation and self-expression
Emerald - supports compassion, trust and forgiveness, opens the heart space
Diopside - offers perspective and boosts creativity, great for manifesting visions

## MOON AFFIRMATION

I believe in myself and have confidence in my abilities. My intentions, hopes, and wishes will be reality because I have the power within me to make it happen.

## MOON RITUAL

This moon is in a growth phase and is an exciting time for positive changes in your life. This moon brings growth, luck and love. Carry a Citrine crystal with you to keep you focused and give you confidence to achieve your goals. Review your goals and keep them where you can see them every day.

# WAXING CRESCENT                JAN 3ᴿᴰ - 8ᵀᴴ

INTENTIONS FOR THIS MOON CYCLE:

HOW AM I FEELING DURING THIS MOON PHASE?

WHERE DO I FIND INSPIRATION? WHY?

WHAT IS MY BODY FEELING RIGHT NOW?

# FIRST QUARTER  JAN 9TH

## MOON IN ARIES

The moon in Aries can cause you to feel more impulsive, direct and powerful. When combined with the First Quarter moon, you will start taking action. This moon will spark your desires and passions. You will feel a burst of momentum to attack your goals headfirst! Take advantage of this time for great change.

## CRYSTALS FOR THIS MOON

Carnelian - great for motivation, courage and inspiration
Blue Lace Agate - a soothing, calming stone for peace
Lapis Lazuli - helps to open the third eye for heightened intuition

## MOON AFFIRMATION

I am taking action to move toward my dreams by using courage and creativity. I will also remember to take time to care for myself.

## MOON RITUAL

Use your Carnelian to create an elixir and sip on it throughout these two days. Place the stone next to a glass of filtered water and leave it by the window to soak up the moon's energy overnight. Say your intentions out loud during this process.

# FIRST QUARTER                                JAN 9TH

The First Quarter Moon represents a period of growth and action.

ACTION ITEMS FOR THIS MOON CYCLE:




HOW AM I FEELING DURING THIS MOON PHASE?




HOW HAVE I BEEN TAKING ACTION TOWARDS MY GOALS?




ARE MY ACTIONS ALIGNED WITH THE INTENTIONS I HAVE SET FOR MYSELF?

# WAXING GIBBOUS          JAN 10TH-16TH

The Waxing Gibbous Moon represents a period of refining and nurturing your goals, hopes and dreams.

10TH-12TH IN TAURUS
13TH-14TH IN GEMINI
15TH-16TH IN CANCER

## CRYSTALS FOR THIS MOON

Fluorite - activates all Chakras and helps you to find your divine calling
Citrine - attracts success, prosperity and magic; boosts confidence and mental clarity
Pyrite - helps with motivation and taking action toward goals
Tigers Eye - invites good luck, blocks bad luck and negative energies

## MOON AFFIRMATION

I have planted the seeds that will bring me closer to my hopes and dreams. I let positive thoughts grow in my mind and open my heart to all the good things that are coming my way. I see my goals clearly and I feel them manifesting.

## MOON RITUAL

This is the best time to work on yourself and use this amazing healing energy. Push yourself to do more than usual. This is a good time to refine and improve. Carry Pyrite to keep you motivated and take action before the waning phase begins.

# WAXING GIBBOUS         JAN 10?? - 16??

INTENTIONS I WANT TO NURTURE DURING
THIS MOON CYCLE:




HOW AM I FEELING DURING THIS MOON PHASE?




WHICH GOALS AM I MOST EXCITED ABOUT?




WHAT IS WORKING FOR ME? WHAT IS NOT?
HOW CAN I IMPROVE?

# FULL WOLF MOON        JAN 17TH

The Full Moon represents a time to harvest your intentions that have been set and making sure they materialize. This Full Moon was known by early Native American tribes as the Full Wolf Moon because this was the time of year when hungry wolf packs howled outside their camps.

## MOON IN CANCER

Celebrating the Full Wolf Moon combined with the beginning of the new year is exciting. This is your chance for a fresh start and a new perspective on your life. The Full Wolf Moon is a great time to practice self-care, mindfulness and meditation. This Cancer moon will be a powerful and emotional time. You should focus on cleansing and purifying your energy and doing healing work on your emotions. If you are Cancer, you will feel a stronger effect.

## FULL MOON CRYSTALS

Cleanse your crystals in this full moon. Leave them in the moonlight for two nights to clear any absorbed energies. The best crystals to use for this Cancer Full Moon are: Carnelian, Moonstone, and Opal. Clear Quartz is also a very powerful crystal to help balance your Chakras during a Full Moon. Set your intentions for joy, creativity, and balanced emotions.

## FULL MOON RITUAL

This is the best time to reflect on your goals for this year. Write down some realistic goals you want to achieve. What do you want to improve in your life? Start a gratitude journal if you don't already have one. Create a vision board. Make a Clear Quartz elixir by putting the stone in distilled water and letting it soak up the moonlight. Drink the elixir after the Full Moon.

# FULL MOON        JAN 17TH

The Full Moon represents a time to harvest your intentions that have been set and making sure they materialize. You can feel the effects of the moon up to a week before and after it occurs.

## WHAT EMOTIONS AM I FEELING TODAY?

## WHAT DOES MY SOUL NEED?

## WHAT HAVE I BEEN NEGLECTING?

## WHAT AREAS OF MY LIFE FEEL OUT OF ALIGNMENT?

# WANING GIBBOUS        JAN 18TH-24TH

The Waning Gibbous Moon represents a period of introspection and gratitude. This is also a time to set intentions and declutter your life.

18TH-19TH IN LEO
20TH-22ND IN VIRGO
23RD-24TH IN LIBRA

## CRYSTALS FOR THIS MOON
Smoky Quartz - Root Chakra, Grounding
Malachite - Cleanse, Purify, Promote positive energy & gratitude
Blue Calcite - Clears negativity and encourages rest & relaxation
Azurite - Strengthens your intuition and psychic abilities
Unakite Jasper - Opens your heart space and brings energy of love

## MOON AFFIRMATION
I am grounded and able to make good decisions. I will be realistic when setting my intentions and goals. I am filled with gratitude for everything that I have.

## MOON RITUAL
Cleanse your home using Palo Santo or Sage. This will make room for positivity in your life and let go of the negativity. Think about anything you need to let go of in your life. Keep a crystal close while you write a list down on paper and create your action plan to let these things go.

# WANING GIBBOUS                    JAN 18TH–24TH

WHAT AM I GRATEFUL FOR?




HOW AM I FEELING DURING THIS MOON PHASE?




HOW CAN I IMPROVE MY MINDFULNESS?




WHAT NEW THINGS HAVE I LEARNED ABOUT MYSELF THIS CYCLE?

# LAST QUARTER                              JAN 25™

## MOON IN SCORPIO

This moon is going to bring some attitude with it. You may begin to feel more curious, so dig deep, investigate and use this creative energy. Be careful not to be too obsessed, because a Scorpio moon can cause major obsession. You will also feel more focused, sexual and intensely emotional. Make sure to block out any past emotional resentments in order to keep your mood stable. This is a great time to cleanse any past emotional debris, do psychic work, and transform yourself.

## CRYSTALS FOR THIS MOON

Black Obsidian - Cleanses aura, removes negative energy blockages
Lapis Lazuli - Good for self-awareness and revealing inner truth
Clear Quartz - Helps you move toward your deepest desires in life

## MOON AFFIRMATION

I release all blockages that are preventing me from moving forward in abundance. Negative energy will not hold me back.

## MOON RITUAL

Spend time in nature and work on grounding yourself. Take action and release all negative behaviors. Carry your obsidian to protect you from negativity. Burn or carry Geranium oil with you to rebuild your energy after releasing the negativity.

# LAST QUARTER                                    JAN 25<sup>TH</sup>

The Last (Third) Quarter Moon represents a period of release and self-assessment. Cleanse any mental and physical obstacles through organization and meditation.

WHAT HABITS ARE STOPPING ME FROM REACHING MY GOALS?

HOW AM I FEELING DURING THIS MOON PHASE?

WHAT COULD I HAVE DONE DIFFERENTLY DURING THIS CYCLE?

WHAT AM I HOLDING ON TO THAT NEEDS TO BE RELEASED?

# WANING CRESCENT      JAN 26TH-31ST

The Waning Crescent Moon represents a period of surrender and a time for rest.

26TH IN SCORPIO
27TH-28TH IN SAGITTARIUS
29TH-30TH IN CAPRICORN
31ST IN AQUARIUS

## CRYSTALS FOR THIS MOON

Bloodstone - helps to embrace the transformation you have been through
Rainbow Fluorite - helps to balance emotions during this up and down period
Black Tourmaline - Grounds your spirit, deflects negative energies
Petalite - Brings peace and calm, supports working with Spirit and angel guides
Black Obsidian - Gently grounding and protective, strengthens your aura field

## MOON AFFIRMATION

I remain centered while my emotions change, and I release any emotions I have been repressing. I can remain balanced and take time to care for myself.

## MOON RITUAL

This moon marks the end of the healing cycle. Think of anything you need to do to complete this cycle before the next one begins. Be gentle to yourself and practice some self-care during this time. Do anything that relaxes you and helps you to feel calm and secure. Take a bath with your crystals surrounding you.

# WANING CRESCENT  JAN 26TH-31ST

HOW CAN I IMPROVE MY SELF-CARE?

HOW AM I FEELING DURING THIS MOON PHASE?

WHAT DO I NEED TO DO FOR MYSELF?

IS THERE ANYTHING IN MY LIFE HOLDING ME BACK? HOW CAN I LET GO?

# MONTH-END REFLECTION

WHAT GOALS DID I ACHIEVE THIS PAST MONTH?

WHAT ARE SOME THINGS I CAN IMPROVE ON NEXT MONTH?

WHAT ARE THE THREE MOST IMPORTANT THINGS I LEARNED THIS PAST MONTH?

WHAT DO I LOOK FORWARD TO ACHIEVING NEXT MONTH?

# FEBRUARY 2022

1st NEW MOON
2nd-7th WAXING CRESCENT
8th FIRST QUARTER
9th-15th WAXING GIBBOUS
16th FULL MOON
17th-22nd WANING GIBBOUS
23rd LAST QUARTER
24th-28th WANING CRESCENT

(EST USA Time Zone)

# NEW MOON GUIDE        FEB 1ST

The Moon will be located on the same side of the Earth as the Sun which means you cannot see the moon from Earth.

## MOON IN AQUARIUS

The New Moon in Aquarius is a good time to focus on positive energy and new goals with a fresh start. This new moon is a very intellectual one. Look to the future with a new positive outlook on life. Recognize that some level of detachment from habits of the past will help you break away from destructive behaviors that are holding you back. If you are an Aquarius, you will feel a stronger effect.

## NEW MOON CRYSTALS

Charge your crystals in this new moon. Leave them out for two nights. You cannot see the moon at this time, but the cleansing is still powerful.
Crystals that are powerful in the Aquarius New Moon are:
Garnet, Amethyst, Amber, Hematite, and Clear Quartz. Set your intentions for making the world a better place and sharing your uniqueness with the world.

## NEW MOON RITUAL

Use sage to smudge your space for the ritual. Light a candle. Write down your intentions for the next month on a piece of paper. Meditate on your intentions. In a safe place, light the paper on fire to send your intentions into the universe. Then, take a few moments for yourself. Read a book, take a quiet walk, pray, meditate or rest. Take your crystals to bed with you tonight. You can feel the effects of the moon up to a week before and after it occurs.

# NEW MOON          FEB 1ˢᵀ

The New Moon represents a fresh start and new beginnings.

GOALS FOR THIS MOON CYCLE:




HOW AM I FEELING DURING THIS MOON PHASE?




HOW CAN I EXPERIENCE MORE JOY AND PEACE?




WHAT IN MY LIFE NEEDS NOURISHMENT?

# WAXING CRESCENT  FEB 2ND-7TH

The Waxing Crescent Moon Phase represents setting intentions. This moon phase also represents positive changes in your emotional state.

2ND-3RD IN PISCES
4TH-6TH IN ARIES
7TH IN TAURUS

## CRYSTALS FOR THIS MOON

Amethyst - brings inspiration, awakens insight and intuition
Citrine - stimulates the brain, promotes motivation and self-expression
Emerald - supports compassion, trust and forgiveness, opens the heart space
Diopside - offers perspective and boosts creativity, great for manifesting visions

## MOON AFFIRMATION

I believe in myself and have confidence in my abilities. My intentions, hopes, and wishes will be reality because I have the power within me to make it happen.

## MOON RITUAL

This moon is in a growth phase and is an exciting time for positive changes in your life. This moon brings growth, luck and love. Carry a Citrine crystal with you to keep you focused and give you confidence to achieve your goals. Review your goals and keep them where you can see them every day.

# WAXING CRESCENT     FEB 2ND-7TH

INTENTIONS FOR THIS MOON CYCLE:




HOW AM I FEELING DURING THIS MOON PHASE?




WHERE DO I FIND INSPIRATION? WHY?




WHAT IS MY BODY FEELING RIGHT NOW?

# FIRST QUARTER                         FEB 8th

### MOON IN TAURUS

You may find yourself more interested in music today due to the energy from Taurus, so turn it up! Taurus also likes comfort, so you should try to take a moment to rest and don't make any big decisions or changes. Because this is a grounding moon energy, you will slow down and dig deeper roots. Now is a good time to focus on preparing delicious food, planting in your garden, or taking a long bubble bath. Choose activities that you love the most!

### CRYSTALS FOR THIS MOON

Carnelian - great for motivation, courage and inspiration
Blue Lace Agate - a soothing, calming stone for peace
Lapis Lazuli - helps to open the third eye for heightened intuition

### MOON AFFIRMATION

I am taking action to move toward my dreams by using courage and creativity.
I will also remember to take time to care for myself during this cycle.

### MOON RITUAL

Use your Carnelian to create an elixir and sip on it throughout these two days. Place the stone next to a glass of filtered water and leave it by the window to soak up the moon's energy overnight. Say your intentions out loud during this process.

# FIRST QUARTER                FEB 8TH

The First Quarter Moon represents a period of growth and action.

ACTION ITEMS FOR THIS MOON CYCLE:

HOW AM I FEELING DURING THIS MOON PHASE?

HOW HAVE I BEEN TAKING ACTION TOWARDS MY GOALS?

ARE MY ACTIONS ALIGNED WITH THE INTENTIONS I HAVE SET FOR MYSELF?

# WAXING GIBBOUS       FEB 9TH-15TH

The Waxing Gibbous Moon represents a period of refining and nurturing your goals, hopes and dreams.

9TH-11TH IN GEMINI
12TH-13TH IN CANCER
14TH-15TH IN LEO

## CRYSTALS FOR THIS MOON

Fluorite - activates all Chakras and helps you to find your divine calling
Citrine - attracts success, prosperity and magic; boosts confidence and mental clarity
Pyrite - helps with motivation and taking action toward goals
Tigers Eye - invites good luck, blocks bad luck and negative energies

## MOON AFFIRMATION

I have planted the seeds that will bring me closer to my hopes and dreams. I let positive thoughts grow in my mind and open my heart to all the good things that are coming my way. I see my goals clearly and I feel them manifesting.

## MOON RITUAL

This is the best time to work on yourself and use this amazing healing energy. Push yourself to do more than usual. This is a good time to refine and improve. Carry Pyrite to keep you motivated and take action before the waning phase begins.

# WAXING GIBBOUS

### FEB 9TH–15TH

INTENTIONS I WANT TO NURTURE DURING THIS MOON CYCLE:

HOW AM I FEELING DURING THIS MOON PHASE?

WHICH GOALS AM I MOST EXCITED ABOUT?

WHAT IS WORKING FOR ME? WHAT IS NOT? HOW CAN I IMPROVE?

# FULL SNOW MOON                              FEB 16TH

The Full Moon represents a time to harvest your intentions that have been set and making sure they materialize. This Full Moon was known by early Native American tribes as the Full Snow Moon because the heaviest snows usually fell during this time of the year.

## MOON IN LEO

This Leo moon will bring out your creative and courageous side. You will feel encouraged to shine and show your unique abilities. Your creativity will bloom. This moon is about finding your confidence. Look into what you do have in your life to find happiness. Honor yourself. Look within and pour your energy into areas of yourself that will be worthwhile and bring you the most joy. If you are Leo, you will feel a stronger effect.

## FULL MOON CRYSTALS

Cleanse your crystals in this full moon. Leave them in the moonlight for two nights to clear any absorbed energies. The best crystals to use for this Leo Full Moon are: Citrine, Carnelian, Kunzite, and Black Tourmaline. Clear Quartz is also a very powerful crystal to help balance your Chakras during a Full Moon. Set your intentions for release, creativity, and protection.

## FULL MOON RITUAL

When you wake up, practice positive affirmations, highlighting the things you love most about yourself. Then, make a list of everything you want to attract in your life. Meditate and focus on your breathing. Say "I honor myself" as you breathe in and say "I am that which I seek" as you breathe out.

# FULL MOON                          FEB 16TH

The Full Moon represents a time to harvest your intentions that have been set and making sure they materialize. You can feel the effects of the moon up to a week before and after it occurs.

## WHAT EMOTIONS AM I FEELING TODAY?

## WHAT DOES MY SOUL NEED?

## WHAT HAVE I BEEN NEGLECTING?

## WHAT AREAS OF MY LIFE FEEL OUT OF ALIGNMENT?

# WANING GIBBOUS      FEB 17TH–22ND

The Waning Gibbous Moon represents a period of introspection and gratitude. This is also a time to set intentions and declutter your life.

17TH–18TH IN VIRGO
19TH–20TH IN LIBRA
21ST–22ND IN SCORPIO

## CRYSTALS FOR THIS MOON
Smoky Quartz – Root Chakra, Grounding
Malachite – Cleanse, Purify, Promote positive energy & gratitude
Blue Calcite – Clears negativity and encourages rest & relaxation
Azurite – Strengthens your intuition and psychic abilities
Unakite Jasper – Opens your heart space and brings energy of love

## MOON AFFIRMATION
I am grounded and able to make good decisions. I will be realistic when setting my intentions and goals. I am filled with gratitude for everything that I have.

## MOON RITUAL
Cleanse your home using Palo Santo or Sage. This will make room for positivity in your life and let go of the negativity. Think about anything you need to let go of in your life. Keep a crystal close while you write a list down on paper and create your action plan to let these things go.

# WANING GIBBOUS                FEB 17<sup>TH</sup>-22<sup>ND</sup>

WHAT AM I GRATEFUL FOR?



HOW AM I FEELING DURING THIS MOON PHASE?



HOW CAN I IMPROVE MY MINDFULNESS?



WHAT NEW THINGS HAVE I LEARNED ABOUT MYSELF THIS CYCLE?

# LAST QUARTER                          FEB 23ᴿᴰ

## MOON IN SAGITTARIUS

This moon brings an active spirit. You will have an open mind, soul, and attitude and won't be able to sit still. Sagittarius brings the need to explore. You will feel the need to travel, study new things, be spontaneous, and spend time with new people in new places. This is the best time to work on any legal matters, travel, and discover hidden truths. Take a new class to explore your abilities or simply use this moon's energy to open your mind further.

## CRYSTALS FOR THIS MOON

Black Obsidian - Cleanses aura, removes negative energy blockages
Lapis Lazuli - Good for self-awareness and revealing inner truth
Clear Quartz - Helps you move toward your deepest desires in life

## MOON AFFIRMATION

I release all blockages that are preventing me from moving forward in abundance. Negative energy will not hold me back.

## MOON RITUAL

Spend time in nature and work on grounding yourself. Take action and release all negative behaviors. Carry your obsidian to protect you from negativity. Burn or carry Geranium oil with you to rebuild your energy after releasing the negativity.

# LAST QUARTER               FEB 23ʳᴰ

The Last (Third) Quarter Moon represents a period of release and self-assessment. Cleanse any mental and physical obstacles through organization and meditation.

WHAT HABITS ARE STOPPING ME FROM REACHING MY GOALS?

HOW AM I FEELING DURING THIS MOON PHASE?

WHAT COULD I HAVE DONE DIFFERENTLY DURING THIS CYCLE?

WHAT AM I HOLDING ON TO THAT NEEDS TO BE RELEASED?

# WANING CRESCENT      FEB 24TH-28TH

The Waning Crescent Moon represents a period of surrender and a time for rest.

24TH IN SAGITTARIUS
25TH-27TH IN CAPRICORN
28TH IN AQUARIUS

## CRYSTALS FOR THIS MOON

Bloodstone - helps to embrace the transformation you have been through
Rainbow Fluorite - helps to balance emotions during this up and down period
Black Tourmaline - Grounds your spirit, deflects negative energies
Petalite - Brings peace and calm, supports working with Spirit and angel guides
Black Obsidian - Gently grounding and protective, strengthens your aura field

## MOON AFFIRMATION

I remain centered while my emotions change, and I release any emotions I have been repressing. I can remain balanced and take time to care for myself.

## MOON RITUAL

This moon marks the end of the healing cycle. Think of anything you need to do to complete this cycle before the next one begins. Be gentle to yourself and practice some self-care during this time. Do anything that relaxes you and helps you to feel calm and secure. Take a bath with your crystals surrounding you.

# WANING CRESCENT          FEB 24ᵀᴴ-28ᵀᴴ

HOW CAN I IMPROVE MY SELF-CARE?



HOW AM I FEELING DURING THIS MOON PHASE?



WHAT DO I NEED TO DO FOR MYSELF?



IS THERE ANYTHING IN MY LIFE HOLDING ME BACK?
HOW CAN I LET GO?

# MONTH-END REFLECTION

WHAT GOALS DID I ACHIEVE THIS PAST MONTH?

WHAT ARE SOME THINGS I CAN IMPROVE ON NEXT MONTH?

WHAT ARE THE THREE MOST IMPORTANT THINGS I LEARNED THIS PAST MONTH?

WHAT DO I LOOK FORWARD TO ACHIEVING NEXT MONTH?

# MARCH 2022

1st WANING CRESCENT
2nd NEW MOON
3rd-9th WAXING CRESCENT
10th FIRST QUARTER
11th-17th WAXING GIBBOUS
18th FULL MOON
19th-24th WANING GIBBOUS
25th LAST QUARTER
26th-31st WANING CRESCENT

MARCH EQUINOX
March 20th

(EST USA Time Zone)

# WANING CRESCENT — MAR 1ˢᵀ

The Waning Crescent Moon represents a period of surrender and a time for rest.

## IN AQUARIUS

## CRYSTALS FOR THIS MOON

Bloodstone - helps to embrace the transformation you have been through
Rainbow Fluorite - helps to balance emotions during this up and down period
Black Tourmaline - Grounds your spirit, deflects negative energies
Petalite - Brings peace and calm, supports working with Spirit and angel guides
Black Obsidian - Gently grounding and protective, strengthens your aura field

## MOON AFFIRMATION

I remain centered while my emotions change, and I release any emotions I have been repressing. I can remain balanced and take time to care for myself.

## MOON RITUAL

This moon marks the end of the healing cycle. Think of anything you need to do to complete this cycle before the next one begins. Be gentle to yourself and practice some self-care during this time. Do anything that relaxes you and helps you to feel calm and secure. Take a bath with your crystals surrounding you.

# WANING CRESCENT  MAR 1ˢᵗ

HOW CAN I IMPROVE MY SELF-CARE?

HOW AM I FEELING DURING THIS MOON PHASE?

WHAT DO I NEED TO DO FOR MYSELF?

IS THERE ANYTHING IN MY LIFE HOLDING ME BACK?
HOW CAN I LET GO?

# NEW MOON GUIDE  MAR 2ND

The Moon will be located on the same side of the Earth as the Sun which means you cannot see the moon from Earth.

## MOON IN PISCES

The New Moon in Pisces has the greatest sensitivity and perceptiveness of surroundings. Channel your energy in a positive way and find ways to unwind and relax. Your dreams and intuition may be heightened during this time. This moon also brings feelings of kindness, compassion, hopefulness and dreams. This is a good time for letting go of your anxieties and finding ways to unwind during times of stress and tension. If you are a Pisces, you will feel a stronger effect.

## NEW MOON CRYSTALS

Charge your crystals in this new moon. Leave them out for two nights. You cannot see the moon at this time, but the cleansing is still powerful. Crystals that are powerful in the Pisces New Moon are: Aquamarine, Jade, Obsidian, Aventurine, Kunzite and Sunstone. Set your intentions for letting go of what is holding you back and caring for yourself with compassion and forgiveness.

## NEW MOON RITUAL

Use sage to smudge your space for the ritual. Light a candle. Write down your intentions for the next month on a piece of paper. Meditate on your intentions. In a safe place, light the paper on fire to send your intentions into the universe. Then, take a few moments for yourself. Read a book, take a quiet walk, pray, meditate or rest. Take your crystals to bed with you tonight. You can feel the effects of the moon up to a week before and after it occurs.

# NEW MOON                     MAR 2ND

The New Moon represents a fresh start and new beginnings.

GOALS FOR THIS MOON CYCLE:

HOW AM I FEELING DURING THIS MOON PHASE?

HOW CAN I EXPERIENCE MORE JOY AND PEACE?

WHAT IN MY LIFE NEEDS NOURISHMENT?

# WAXING CRESCENT          MAR 3RD - 9TH

The Waxing Crescent Moon Phase represents setting intentions. This moon phase also represents positive changes in your emotional state.

3RD IN PISCES
4TH - 5TH IN ARIES
6TH - 8TH IN TAURUS
9TH IN GEMINI

## CRYSTALS FOR THIS MOON

Amethyst - brings inspiration, awakens insight and intuition
Citrine - stimulates the brain, promotes motivation and self-expression
Emerald - supports compassion, trust and forgiveness, opens the heart space
Diopside - offers perspective and boosts creativity, great for manifesting visions

## MOON AFFIRMATION

I believe in myself and have confidence in my abilities. My intentions, hopes, and wishes will be reality because I have the power within me to make it happen.

## MOON RITUAL

This moon is in a growth phase and is an exciting time for positive changes in your life. This moon brings growth, luck and love. Carry a Citrine crystal with you to keep you focused and give you confidence to achieve your goals. Review your goals and keep them where you can see them every day.

# WAXING CRESCENT  MAR 3ʳᵈ - 9ᵀᴴ

INTENTIONS FOR THIS MOON CYCLE:

HOW AM I FEELING DURING THIS MOON PHASE?

WHERE DO I FIND INSPIRATION? WHY?

WHAT IS MY BODY FEELING RIGHT NOW?

# FIRST QUARTER                    MAR 10TH

## MOON IN GEMINI

This moon is a good time for networking, communicating, and learning. Focus on brainstorming new ideas, meditating, and using expression in writing. You may struggle with concentration right now, so it is best to focus on the highest priorities. Speak to your plants, trim them but avoid planting. Go on a short trip. Take a trip to the library or bookstore. Spend time with your family. Make a list of what you would like to learn that would make your life easier. Keep communication open with others and release yourself from any negative thoughts.

## CRYSTALS FOR THIS MOON

Carnelian - great for motivation, courage and inspiration
Blue Lace Agate - a soothing, calming stone for peace
Lapis Lazuli - helps to open the third eye for heightened intuition

## MOON AFFIRMATION

I am taking action to move toward my dreams by using courage and creativity. I will also remember to take time to care for myself during this cycle.

## MOON RITUAL

Use your Carnelian to create an elixir and sip on it throughout these two days. Place the stone next to a glass of filtered water and leave it by the window to soak up the moon's energy overnight. Say your intentions out loud during this process.

# FIRST QUARTER

MAR 10TH

The First Quarter Moon represents a period of growth and action.

ACTION ITEMS FOR THIS MOON CYCLE:

HOW AM I FEELING DURING THIS MOON PHASE?

HOW HAVE I BEEN TAKING ACTION TOWARDS MY GOALS?

ARE MY ACTIONS ALIGNED WITH THE INTENTIONS I HAVE SET FOR MYSELF?

# WAXING GIBBOUS      MAR 11TH- 17TH

The Waxing Gibbous Moon represents a period of refining and nurturing your goals, hopes and dreams.

11TH- 13TH IN CANCER
14TH- 15TH IN LEO
16TH- 17TH IN VIRGO

## CRYSTALS FOR THIS MOON

Fluorite - activates all Chakras and helps you to find your divine calling
Citrine - attracts success, prosperity and magic; boosts confidence and mental clarity
Pyrite - helps with motivation and taking action toward goals
Tigers Eye - invites good luck, blocks bad luck and negative energies

## MOON AFFIRMATION

I have planted the seeds that will bring me closer to my hopes and dreams. I let positive thoughts grow in my mind and open my heart to all the good things that are coming my way. I see my goals clearly and I feel them manifesting.

## MOON RITUAL

This is the best time to work on yourself and use this amazing healing energy. Push yourself to do more than usual. This is a good time to refine and improve. Carry Pyrite to keep you motivated and take action before the waning phase begins.

# WAXING GIBBOUS        MAR 11TH- 17TH

INTENTIONS I WANT TO NURTURE DURING
THIS MOON CYCLE:




HOW AM I FEELING DURING THIS MOON PHASE?




WHICH GOALS AM I MOST EXCITED ABOUT?




WHAT IS WORKING FOR ME? WHAT IS NOT?
HOW CAN I IMPROVE?

# FULL WORM MOON        MAR 18TH

The Full Moon represents a time to harvest your intentions that have been set and making sure they materialize. This Full Moon was known by early Native American tribes as the Full Worm Moon because this was the time of year when the ground would begin to soften, and the earthworms would appear.

## MOON IN LIBRA

This moon will help you with speaking your truth, pursuing justice and resolving any conflicts in your life. You will experience an increase in self-awareness, self-examination and interaction with others. This is a good time to beautify, create, and find your balance in life. Express yourself by letting your artistic side out. Focus on spiritual and emotional balance. If you are a Libra, you will feel a stronger effect.

## FULL MOON CRYSTALS

Cleanse your crystals in this full moon. Leave them in the moonlight for two nights to clear any absorbed energies. The best crystals to use for this Libra Full Moon are: Ametrine, Labradorite, Jade and Rose Quartz. Clear Quartz is also a very powerful crystal to help balance your Chakras during a Full Moon. Set your intentions to focus on relationships, balance, and harmony in your life.

## FULL MOON RITUAL

Cleanse the air by burning sage, incense or diffusing essential oils. Ground yourself by taking slow, deep breaths. Meditate upon any areas in your life that are feeling out of balance. Breathe into these areas of your life as you send them love + healing. Once you know what your intention is, write it down on paper and place it outside in the full moon with your crystals.

# FULL MOON           MAR 18TH

The Full Moon represents a time to harvest your intentions that have been set and making sure they materialize. You can feel the effects of the moon up to a week before and after it occurs.

## WHAT EMOTIONS AM I FEELING TODAY?

## WHAT DOES MY SOUL NEED?

## WHAT HAVE I BEEN NEGLECTING?

## WHAT AREAS OF MY LIFE FEEL OUT OF ALIGNMENT?

# WANING GIBBOUS  MAR 19TH-24TH

The Waning Gibbous Moon represents a period of introspection and gratitude. This is also a time to set intentions and declutter your life.

19TH IN LIBRA
20TH-22ND IN SCORPIO
23RD-24TH IN SAGITTARIUS

## CRYSTALS FOR THIS MOON
Smoky Quartz - Root Chakra, Grounding
Malachite - Cleanse, Purify, Promote positive energy & gratitude
Blue Calcite - Clears negativity and encourages rest & relaxation
Azurite - Strengthens your intuition and psychic abilities
Unakite Jasper - Opens your heart space and brings energy of love

## MOON AFFIRMATION
I am grounded and able to make good decisions. I will be realistic when setting my intentions and goals. I am filled with gratitude for everything that I have.

## MOON RITUAL
Cleanse your home using Palo Santo or Sage. This will make room for positivity in your life and let go of the negativity. Think about anything you need to let go of in your life. Keep a crystal close while you write a list down on paper and create your action plan to let these things go.

# WANING GIBBOUS         MAR 19TH-24TH

WHAT AM I GRATEFUL FOR?

HOW AM I FEELING DURING THIS MOON PHASE?

HOW CAN I IMPROVE MY MINDFULNESS?

WHAT NEW THINGS HAVE I LEARNED ABOUT MYSELF THIS CYCLE?

# LAST QUARTER                    MAR 25TH

## MOON IN CAPRICORN

When the moon is in Capricorn, you will feel more productive and serious. This is because Capricorn is an Earth sign, and this sign craves substance. With the extra patience and discipline this moon brings, you should focus on overcoming any difficult obstacles, finalizing business plans, and manifesting your goals. Your ambitious side will feel more intense and now is the best time to dig deep and make sure you are ready to achieve your goals.

## CRYSTALS FOR THIS MOON

Black Obsidian - Cleanses aura, removes negative energy blockages
Lapis Lazuli - Good for self-awareness and revealing inner truth
Clear Quartz - Helps you move toward your deepest desires in life

## MOON AFFIRMATION

I release all blockages that are preventing me from moving forward in abundance. Negative energy will not hold me back.

## MOON RITUAL

Spend time in nature and work on grounding yourself. Take action and release all negative behaviors. Carry your obsidian to protect you from negativity. Burn or carry Geranium oil with you to rebuild your energy after releasing the negativity.

# LAST QUARTER                    MAR 25TH

The Last (Third) Quarter Moon represents a period of release and self-assessment. Cleanse any mental and physical obstacles through organization and meditation.

WHAT HABITS ARE STOPPING ME FROM REACHING MY GOALS?

HOW AM I FEELING DURING THIS MOON PHASE?

WHAT COULD I HAVE DONE DIFFERENTLY DURING THIS CYCLE?

WHAT AM I HOLDING ON TO THAT NEEDS TO BE RELEASED?

# WANING CRESCENT    MAR 26ᵀᴴ-31ˢᵀ

The Waning Crescent Moon represents a period of surrender and a time for rest.

26ᵀᴴ IN CAPRICORN
27ᵀᴴ-28ᵀᴴ IN AQUARIUS
29ᵀᴴ-30ᵀᴴ IN PISCES
31ˢᵀ IN ARIES

## CRYSTALS FOR THIS MOON

Bloodstone - helps to embrace the transformation you have been through
Rainbow Fluorite - helps to balance emotions during this up and down period
Black Tourmaline - Grounds your spirit, deflects negative energies
Petalite - Brings peace and calm, supports working with Spirit and angel guides
Black Obsidian - Gently grounding and protective, strengthens your aura field

## MOON AFFIRMATION

I remain centered while my emotions change, and I release any emotions I have been repressing. I can remain balanced and take time to care for myself.

## MOON RITUAL

This moon marks the end of the healing cycle. Think of anything you need to do to complete this cycle before the next one begins. Be gentle to yourself and practice some self-care during this time. Do anything that relaxes you and helps you to feel calm and secure. Take a bath with your crystals surrounding you.

# WANING CRESCENT       MAR 26TH-31ST

HOW CAN I IMPROVE MY SELF-CARE?




HOW AM I FEELING DURING THIS MOON PHASE?




WHAT DO I NEED TO DO FOR MYSELF?




IS THERE ANYTHING IN MY LIFE HOLDING ME BACK?
HOW CAN I LET GO?

# MONTH-END REFLECTION

WHAT GOALS DID I ACHIEVE THIS PAST MONTH?

WHAT ARE SOME THINGS I CAN IMPROVE ON NEXT MONTH?

WHAT ARE THE THREE MOST IMPORTANT THINGS I LEARNED THIS PAST MONTH?

WHAT DO I LOOK FORWARD TO ACHIEVING NEXT MONTH?

# APRIL 2022

1st NEW MOON
2nd-8th WAXING CRESCENT
9th FIRST QUARTER
10th-15th WAXING GIBBOUS
16th FULL MOON
17th-22nd WANING GIBBOUS
23rd LAST QUARTER
24th-29th WANING CRESCENT
30th NEW MOON

PARTIAL SOLAR ECLIPSE
April 30th

(EST USA Time Zone)

# NEW MOON GUIDE　　　　　　APR 1ST

The Moon will be located on the same side of the Earth as the Sun which means you cannot see the moon from Earth.

## MOON IN ARIES

The New Moon in Aries will bring powerful energy that will make you want to take action! Use this boost of energy to get more aggressive with your goals. Use this new momentum to step out of your comfort zone by doing something new. Quick, short activities are most favored during this time, so don't try to take on longer projects just yet. This moon can lead to impulsive behavior, so make sure to do some soul searching first. If you are an Aries, you will feel a stronger effect.

## NEW MOON CRYSTALS

Charge your crystals in this new moon. Leave them out for two nights. You cannot see the moon at this time, but the cleansing is still powerful. Crystals that are powerful in the Aries New Moon are: Aventurine, Azurite, Bloodstone, Citrine, and Fluorite. Set your intentions for self-love, reflection, discarding negative emotions, and speaking your truth.

## NEW MOON RITUAL

Use sage to smudge your space for the ritual. Light a candle. Write down your intentions for the next month on a piece of paper. Meditate on your intentions. In a safe place, light the paper on fire to send your intentions into the universe. Then, take a few moments for yourself. Read a book, take a quiet walk, pray, meditate or rest. Take your crystals to bed with you tonight. You can feel the effects of the moon up to a week before and after it occurs.

# NEW MOON                                APR 1ˢᵀ

The New Moon represents a fresh start and new beginnings.

GOALS FOR THIS MOON CYCLE:




HOW AM I FEELING DURING THIS MOON PHASE?




HOW CAN I EXPERIENCE MORE JOY AND PEACE?




WHAT IN MY LIFE NEEDS NOURISHMENT?

# WAXING CRESCENT          APR 2ND - 8TH

The Waxing Crescent Moon Phase represents setting intentions. This moon phase also represents positive changes in your emotional state.

2ND IN ARIES
3RD - 4TH IN TAURUS
5TH - 6TH IN GEMINI
7TH - 8TH IN CANCER

## CRYSTALS FOR THIS MOON

Amethyst - brings inspiration, awakens insight and intuition
Citrine - stimulates the brain, promotes motivation and self-expression
Emerald - supports compassion, trust and forgiveness, opens the heart space
Diopside - offers perspective and boosts creativity, great for manifesting visions

## MOON AFFIRMATION

I believe in myself and have confidence in my abilities. My intentions, hopes, and wishes will be reality because I have the power within me to make it happen.

## MOON RITUAL

This moon is in a growth phase and is an exciting time for positive changes in your life. This moon brings growth, luck and love. Carry a Citrine crystal with you to keep you focused and give you confidence to achieve your goals. Review your goals and keep them where you can see them every day.

# WAXING CRESCENT APR 2<sup>ND</sup>-8<sup>TH</sup>

INTENTIONS FOR THIS MOON CYCLE:




HOW AM I FEELING DURING THIS MOON PHASE?




WHERE DO I FIND INSPIRATION? WHY?




WHAT IS MY BODY FEELING RIGHT NOW?

# FIRST QUARTER                             APR 9TH

## MOON IN CANCER

This Cancer moon will pull you toward family and you will feel a strong urge to nurture and care for those around you. Now is a time to be surrounded by your loved ones. This moon also brings out kindness and you may spend more time helping others. Use this time to express yourself, perform random acts of kindness, and journal. If you are Cancer, you will feel a stronger effect.

## CRYSTALS FOR THIS MOON

Carnelian - great for motivation, courage and inspiration
Blue Lace Agate - a soothing, calming stone for peace
Lapis Lazuli - helps to open the third eye for heightened intuition

## MOON AFFIRMATION

I am taking action to move toward my dreams by using courage and creativity. I will also remember to take time to care for myself during this cycle.

## MOON RITUAL

Use your Carnelian to create an elixir and sip on it throughout these two days. Place the stone next to a glass of filtered water and leave it by the window to soak up the moon's energy overnight. Say your intentions out loud during this process.

# FIRST QUARTER                                      APR 9TH

The First Quarter Moon represents a period of growth and action.

ACTION ITEMS FOR THIS MOON CYCLE:




HOW AM I FEELING DURING THIS MOON PHASE?




HOW HAVE I BEEN TAKING ACTION TOWARDS MY GOALS?




ARE MY ACTIONS ALIGNED WITH THE INTENTIONS I HAVE SET FOR MYSELF?

# WAXING GIBBOUS      APR 10TH-15TH

The Waxing Gibbous Moon represents a period of refining and nurturing your goals, hopes and dreams.

10TH-11TH IN LEO
12TH-14TH IN VIRGO
15TH IN LIBRA

## CRYSTALS FOR THIS MOON

Fluorite - activates all Chakras and helps you to find your divine calling
Citrine - attracts success, prosperity and magic; boosts confidence and mental clarity
Pyrite - helps with motivation and taking action toward goals
Tigers Eye - invites good luck, blocks bad luck and negative energies

## MOON AFFIRMATION

I have planted the seeds that will bring me closer to my hopes and dreams. I let positive thoughts grow in my mind and open my heart to all the good things that are coming my way. I see my goals clearly and I feel them manifesting.

## MOON RITUAL

This is the best time to work on yourself and use this amazing healing energy. Push yourself to do more than usual. This is a good time to refine and improve. Carry Pyrite to keep you motivated and take action before the waning phase begins.

# WAXING GIBBOUS     APR 10TH - 15TH

INTENTIONS I WANT TO NURTURE DURING
THIS MOON CYCLE:

HOW AM I FEELING DURING THIS MOON PHASE?

WHICH GOALS AM I MOST EXCITED ABOUT?

WHAT IS WORKING FOR ME? WHAT IS NOT?
HOW CAN I IMPROVE?

# FULL PINK MOON                    APR 16TH

The Full Moon represents a time to harvest your intentions that have been set and making sure they materialize. This Full Moon was known by early Native American tribes as the Full Pink Moon because it marked the appearance of the pink moss, which is one of the first spring flowers.

## MOON IN LIBRA

This moon will help you with speaking your truth, pursuing justice and resolving any conflicts in your life. You will experience an increase in self-awareness, self-examination and interaction with others. This is a good time to beautify, create, and find your balance in life. Express yourself by letting your artistic side out. Focus on spiritual and emotional balance. If you are a Libra, you will feel a stronger effect.

## FULL MOON CRYSTALS

Cleanse your crystals in this full moon. Leave them in the moonlight for two nights to clear any absorbed energies. The best crystals to use for this Libra Full Moon are: Ametrine, Labradorite, Jade and Rose Quartz. Clear Quartz is also a very powerful crystal to help balance your Chakras during a Full Moon. Set your intentions to focus on relationships, balance, and harmony in your life.

## FULL MOON RITUAL

On a piece of paper, write down anything you wish to release from your life. On another, write what you are seeking to achieve or manifest. Using a small bowl, go outdoors and light both papers on fire or tear them into pieces. Say "I release what no longer serves me to make room for what I really want". Journal about your thoughts, then meditate using deep breathing.

# FULL MOON  APR 16TH

The Full Moon represents a time to harvest your intentions that have been set and making sure they materialize. You can feel the effects of the moon up to a week before and after it occurs.

WHAT EMOTIONS AM I FEELING TODAY?

WHAT DOES MY SOUL NEED?

WHAT HAVE I BEEN NEGLECTING?

WHAT AREAS OF MY LIFE FEEL OUT OF ALIGNMENT?

# WANING GIBBOUS      APR 17TH–22ND

The Waning Gibbous Moon represents a period of introspection and gratitude. This is also a time to set intentions and declutter your life.

17TH–18TH IN SCORPIO
19TH–20TH IN SAGITTARIUS
21ST–22ND IN CAPRICORN

## CRYSTALS FOR THIS MOON

Smoky Quartz - Root Chakra, Grounding
Malachite - Cleanse, Purify, Promote positive energy & gratitude
Blue Calcite - Clears negativity and encourages rest & relaxation
Azurite - Strengthens your intuition and psychic abilities
Unakite Jasper - Opens your heart space and brings energy of love

## MOON AFFIRMATION

I am grounded and able to make good decisions. I will be realistic when setting my intentions and goals. I am filled with gratitude for everything that I have.

## MOON RITUAL

Cleanse your home using Palo Santo or Sage. This will make room for positivity in your life and let go of the negativity. Think about anything you need to let go of in your life. Keep a crystal close while you write a list down on paper and create your action plan to let these things go.

# WANING GIBBOUS         APR 17ᵀᴴ-22ᴺᴰ

WHAT AM I GRATEFUL FOR?




HOW AM I FEELING DURING THIS MOON PHASE?




HOW CAN I IMPROVE MY MINDFULNESS?




WHAT NEW THINGS HAVE I LEARNED ABOUT MYSELF THIS CYCLE?

# LAST QUARTER            APR 23ᴿᴰ

## MOON IN AQUARIUS

This Last Quarter Moon in Aquarius will bring you out of your comfort zone by convincing you to accept sudden changes of plans or going to an unexpected event. This is a rebellious, impulsive moon! This is a great time for alternative therapies such as energy healing, Reiki, acupuncture, or group gatherings. Free your mind by trying Aquarius Yoga. In meditation, focus on your root chakra to keep you grounded and focused.

## CRYSTALS FOR THIS MOON

Black Obsidian - Cleanses aura, removes negative energy blockages
Lapis Lazuli - Good for self-awareness and revealing inner truth
Clear Quartz - Helps you move toward your deepest desires in life

## MOON AFFIRMATION

I release all blockages that are preventing me from moving forward in abundance. Negative energy will not hold me back.

## MOON RITUAL

Spend time in nature and work on grounding yourself. This can be as simple as walking barefoot on the earth. As you connect with nature, feel your anxieties and fears draining away. Let the power of the earth filter away any negative energy. Carry an obsidian with you to strengthen the grounding effect.

# LAST QUARTER        APR 23RD

The Last (Third) Quarter Moon represents a period of release and self-assessment. Cleanse any mental and physical obstacles through organization and meditation.

WHAT HABITS ARE STOPPING ME FROM REACHING MY GOALS?

HOW AM I FEELING DURING THIS MOON PHASE?

WHAT COULD I HAVE DONE DIFFERENTLY DURING THIS CYCLE?

WHAT AM I HOLDING ON TO THAT NEEDS TO BE RELEASED?

# WANING CRESCENT      APR 24TH-29TH

The Waning Crescent Moon represents a period of surrender and a time for rest.

24TH IN AQUARIUS
25TH-27TH IN PISCES
28TH-29TH IN ARIES

## CRYSTALS FOR THIS MOON

Bloodstone - helps to embrace the transformation you have been through
Rainbow Fluorite - helps to balance emotions during this up and down period
Black Tourmaline - Grounds your spirit, deflects negative energies
Petalite - Brings peace and calm, supports working with Spirit and angel guides
Black Obsidian - Gently grounding and protective, strengthens your aura field

## MOON AFFIRMATION

I remain centered while my emotions change, and I release any emotions I have been repressing. I can remain balanced and take time to care for myself.

## MOON RITUAL

This moon marks the end of the healing cycle. Think of anything you need to do to complete this cycle before the next one begins. Be gentle to yourself and practice some self-care during this time. Do anything that relaxes you and helps you to feel calm and secure. Take a bath with your crystals surrounding you.

# WANING CRESCENT APR 24ᵀᴴ-29ᵀᴴ

HOW CAN I IMPROVE MY SELF-CARE?




HOW AM I FEELING DURING THIS MOON PHASE?




WHAT DO I NEED TO DO FOR MYSELF?




IS THERE ANYTHING IN MY LIFE HOLDING ME BACK?
HOW CAN I LET GO?

# NEW MOON GUIDE                    APR 30TH

The Moon will be located on the same side of the Earth as the Sun which means you cannot see the moon from Earth.

## MOON IN TAURUS

The New Moon in Taurus reminds us to slow down and appreciate everything the material world has to offer. It assists in manifesting our desires and goals in life. It also assists us in finding the necessary tools to make changes. Taurus craves security, so this moon will help you with stability and creating a secure environment in which you can flourish. Use all resources wisely during this phase. If you are a Taurus, you will feel a stronger effect.

## NEW MOON CRYSTALS

Charge your crystals in this new moon. Leave them out for two nights. You cannot see the moon at this time, but the cleansing is still powerful. Crystals that are powerful in the Taurus New Moon are: Malachite, Carnelian, Amazonite, Kunzite and Selenite. Set your intentions for refreshing your self-esteem, easing problems in a relationship, and embracing your path ahead.

## NEW MOON RITUAL

Use sage to smudge your space for the ritual. Light a candle. Write down your intentions for the next month on a piece of paper. Meditate on your intentions. In a safe place, light the paper on fire to send your intentions into the universe. Then, take a few moments for yourself. Read a book, take a quiet walk, pray, meditate or rest. Take your crystals to bed with you tonight. You can feel the effects of the moon up to a week before and after it occurs.

# NEW MOON                    APR 30TH

The New Moon represents a fresh start and new beginnings.

GOALS FOR THIS MOON CYCLE:




HOW AM I FEELING DURING THIS MOON PHASE?




HOW CAN I EXPERIENCE MORE JOY AND PEACE?




WHAT IN MY LIFE NEEDS NOURISHMENT?

# MONTH-END REFLECTION

WHAT GOALS DID I ACHIEVE THIS PAST MONTH?

WHAT ARE SOME THINGS I CAN IMPROVE ON NEXT MONTH?

WHAT ARE THE THREE MOST IMPORTANT THINGS I LEARNED THIS PAST MONTH?

WHAT DO I LOOK FORWARD TO ACHIEVING NEXT MONTH?

# MAY 2022

1st-7th WAXING CRESCENT
8th-9th FIRST QUARTER
10th-15th WAXING GIBBOUS
16th FULL MOON
17th-21st WANING GIBBOUS
22nd LAST QUARTER
23rd-29th WANING CRESCENT
30th NEW MOON
31st WAXING CRESCENT

TOTAL LUNAR ECLIPSE
May 16th

(EST USA Time Zone)

# WAXING CRESCENT      MAY 1ST-7TH

The Waxing Crescent Moon Phase represents setting intentions. This moon phase also represents positive changes in your emotional state.

1ST IN TAURUS
2ND-4TH IN GEMINI
5TH-6TH IN CANCER
7TH IN LEO

## CRYSTALS FOR THIS MOON

Amethyst - brings inspiration, awakens insight and intuition
Citrine - stimulates the brain, promotes motivation and self-expression
Emerald - supports compassion, trust and forgiveness, opens the heart space
Diopside - offers perspective and boosts creativity, great for manifesting visions

## MOON AFFIRMATION

I believe in myself and have confidence in my abilities. My intentions, hopes, and wishes will be reality because I have the power within me to make it happen.

## MOON RITUAL

This moon is in a growth phase and is an exciting time for positive changes in your life. This moon brings growth, luck and love. Carry a Citrine crystal with you to keep you focused and give you confidence to achieve your goals. Review your goals and keep them where you can see them every day.

# WAXING CRESCENT     MAY 1ST-7TH

INTENTIONS FOR THIS MOON CYCLE:

HOW AM I FEELING DURING THIS MOON PHASE?

WHERE DO I FIND INSPIRATION? WHY?

WHAT IS MY BODY FEELING RIGHT NOW?

# FIRST QUARTER       MAY 8TH-9TH

## MOON IN LEO

This Leo moon will bring out your creative and courageous side. You will feel encouraged to shine and show your unique abilities. This moon is about finding your confidence. Be creative and put yourself out there; share a talent with the world. This is a time for an awakening but make sure to stay grounded while exploring your creativity so that you don't lose your focus.
If you are Leo, you will feel a stronger effect.

## CRYSTALS FOR THIS MOON

Carnelian - great for motivation, courage and inspiration
Blue Lace Agate - a soothing, calming stone for peace
Lapis Lazuli - helps to open the third eye for heightened intuition

## MOON AFFIRMATION

I am taking action to move toward my dreams by using courage and creativity.
I will also remember to take time to care for myself during this cycle.

## MOON RITUAL

Use your Carnelian to create an elixir and sip on it throughout these two days. Place the stone next to a glass of filtered water and leave it by the window to soak up the moon's energy overnight. Say your intentions out loud during this process.

# FIRST QUARTER

MAY 8^(TH)-9^(TH)

The First Quarter Moon represents a period of growth and action.

ACTION ITEMS FOR THIS MOON CYCLE:

HOW AM I FEELING DURING THIS MOON PHASE?

HOW HAVE I BEEN TAKING ACTION TOWARDS MY GOALS?

ARE MY ACTIONS ALIGNED WITH THE INTENTIONS I HAVE SET FOR MYSELF?

# WAXING GIBBOUS     MAY 10TH-15TH

The Waxing Gibbous Moon represents a period of refining and nurturing your goals, hopes and dreams.

10TH-11TH  IN VIRGO
12TH-13TH  IN LIBRA
14TH-15TH  IN SCORPIO

## CRYSTALS FOR THIS MOON

Fluorite - activates all Chakras and helps you to find your divine calling
Citrine - attracts success, prosperity and magic; boosts confidence and mental clarity
Pyrite - helps with motivation and taking action toward goals
Tigers Eye - invites good luck, blocks bad luck and negative energies

## MOON AFFIRMATION

I have planted the seeds that will bring me closer to my hopes and dreams. I let positive thoughts grow in my mind and open my heart to all the good things that are coming my way. I see my goals clearly and I feel them manifesting.

## MOON RITUAL

This is the best time to work on yourself and use this amazing healing energy. Push yourself to do more than usual. This is a good time to refine and improve. Carry Pyrite to keep you motivated and take action before the waning phase begins.

# WAXING GIBBOUS                MAY 10^(TH)- 15^(TH)

INTENTIONS I WANT TO NURTURE DURING
THIS MOON CYCLE:

HOW AM I FEELING DURING THIS MOON PHASE?

WHICH GOALS AM I MOST EXCITED ABOUT?

WHAT IS WORKING FOR ME? WHAT IS NOT?
HOW CAN I IMPROVE?

# FULL FLOWER MOON         MAY 16TH

The Full Moon represents a time to harvest your intentions that have been set and making sure they materialize. This Full Moon was known by early Native American tribes as the Full Flower Moon because flowers are abundant during this time. This moon is also combined with a lunar eclipse, which will amplify the effect.

## MOON IN SAGITTARIUS

The Full Flower Moon in Sagittarius combined with the lunar eclipse will increase your intuition and cause you to think more about your life than usual. You will really become focused on healing and learning about your true purpose. Pay close attention to your dreams, because messages and thoughts will come to you as you sleep. If you are a Sagittarius, you will feel a stronger effect.

## FULL MOON CRYSTALS

Cleanse your crystals in this Full Moon. Leave them in the moonlight for two nights to clear any absorbed energies. The best crystals to use for this Sagittarius Full Moon are: Aventurine, Azurite, and Clear Quartz. Clear Quartz is also a very powerful crystal to help balance your Chakras during a Full Moon. Set your intentions to find your own personal truth and philosophy of life.

## FULL MOON RITUAL

Smudge sage or diffuse your favorite essential oil to set the tone. Meditate by letting your intuition guide your session. Journal to free your thoughts, follow your heart and pour your thoughts onto the pages. Check in with yourself on your progress toward your goals. Set your intentions and ask the universe to support you in achieving your goals. Feel the power within you!

# FULL MOON

MAY 16TH

The Full Moon represents a time to harvest your intentions that have been set and making sure they materialize. You can feel the effects of the moon up to a week before and after it occurs.

## WHAT EMOTIONS AM I FEELING TODAY?

## WHAT DOES MY SOUL NEED?

## WHAT HAVE I BEEN NEGLECTING?

## WHAT AREAS OF MY LIFE FEEL OUT OF ALIGNMENT?

# WANING GIBBOUS      MAY 17TH-21ST

The Waning Gibbous Moon represents a period of introspection and gratitude. This is also a time to set intentions and declutter your life.

17TH IN SAGITTARIUS
18TH-19TH IN CAPRICORN
20TH-21ST IN AQUARIUS

## CRYSTALS FOR THIS MOON

Smoky Quartz - Root Chakra, Grounding
Malachite - Cleanse, Purify, Promote positive energy & gratitude
Blue Calcite - Clears negativity and encourages rest & relaxation
Azurite - Strengthens your intuition and psychic abilities
Unakite Jasper - Opens your heart space and brings energy of love

## MOON AFFIRMATION

I am grounded and able to make good decisions. I will be realistic when setting my intentions and goals. I am filled with gratitude for everything that I have.

## MOON RITUAL

Cleanse your home using Palo Santo or Sage. This will make room for positivity in your life and let go of the negativity. Think about anything you need to let go of in your life. Keep a crystal close while you write a list down on paper and create your action plan to let these things go.

# WANING GIBBOUS    MAY 17TH-21ST

WHAT AM I GRATEFUL FOR?

HOW AM I FEELING DURING THIS MOON PHASE?

HOW CAN I IMPROVE MY MINDFULNESS?

WHAT NEW THINGS HAVE I LEARNED ABOUT MYSELF THIS CYCLE?

# LAST QUARTER — MAY 22ND

## MOON IN PISCES

Pisces is a water sign - the element of great feeling. This moon will bring a higher sense of sensitivity and emotions. You will feel stronger empathy for others and show more compassion for human struggles around you. This moon will also cause you to struggle with concentration and you may find yourself feeling a bit dreamy and lazy. Relax in a long bath, spend time near a large body of water (ocean, lake, etc), use your imagination on a new project, or help someone in need.

## CRYSTALS FOR THIS MOON

Black Obsidian - Cleanses aura, removes negative energy blockages
Lapis Lazuli - Good for self-awareness and revealing inner truth
Clear Quartz - Helps you move toward your deepest desires in life

## MOON AFFIRMATION

I release all blockages that are preventing me from moving forward in abundance. Negative energy will not hold me back.

## MOON RITUAL

Spend time in nature and work on grounding yourself. Take action and release all negative behaviors. Carry your obsidian to protect you from negativity. Burn or carry Geranium oil with you to rebuild your energy after releasing the negativity.

# LAST QUARTER                    MAY 22ᴺᴰ

The Last (Third) Quarter Moon represents a period of release and self-assessment. Cleanse any mental and physical obstacles through organization and meditation.

WHAT HABITS ARE STOPPING ME FROM REACHING MY GOALS?

HOW AM I FEELING DURING THIS MOON PHASE?

WHAT COULD I HAVE DONE DIFFERENTLY DURING THIS CYCLE?

WHAT AM I HOLDING ON TO THAT NEEDS TO BE RELEASED?

# WANING CRESCENT     MAY 23RD-29TH

The Waning Crescent Moon represents a period of surrender and a time for rest.

23RD-24TH IN PISCES
25TH-26TH IN ARIES
27TH-29TH IN TAURUS

## CRYSTALS FOR THIS MOON

Bloodstone - helps to embrace the transformation you have been through
Rainbow Fluorite - helps to balance emotions during this up and down period
Black Tourmaline - Grounds your spirit, deflects negative energies
Petalite - Brings peace and calm, supports working with Spirit and angel guides
Black Obsidian - Gently grounding and protective, strengthens your aura field

## MOON AFFIRMATION

I remain centered while my emotions change, and I release any emotions I have been repressing. I can remain balanced and take time to care for myself.

## MOON RITUAL

This moon marks the end of the healing cycle. Think of anything you need to do to complete this cycle before the next one begins. Be gentle to yourself and practice some self-care during this time. Do anything that relaxes you and helps you to feel calm and secure. Take a bath with your crystals surrounding you.

# WANING CRESCENT  MAY 23ʳᴰ-29ᵀᴴ

HOW CAN I IMPROVE MY SELF-CARE?

HOW AM I FEELING DURING THIS MOON PHASE?

WHAT DO I NEED TO DO FOR MYSELF?

IS THERE ANYTHING IN MY LIFE HOLDING ME BACK?
HOW CAN I LET GO?

# NEW MOON GUIDE          MAY 30TH

The Moon will be located on the same side of the Earth as the Sun which means you cannot see the moon from Earth.

## MOON IN GEMINI

The New Moon in Gemini is a moon that forces change and self-expression. You may feel more comfortable with making changes at this time. You may also feel a stronger urge for self-expression. This moon will help to provide you with more clarity. Trust your intuition during this time and be open to new ideas that come to mind. Gemini brings new beginnings by offering you the opportunity to free yourself from outside influences as well. If you are a Gemini, you will feel a stronger effect.

## NEW MOON CRYSTALS

Charge your crystals in this new moon. Leave them out for two nights. You cannot see the moon at this time, but the cleansing is still powerful. Crystals that are powerful in the Gemini New Moon are: Celestite, Moonstone, Rhodochrosite, and Blue Kyanite. Set your intentions for unconditional love, removing emotional toxins, and trusting your intuition while embracing change.

## NEW MOON RITUAL

Use sage to smudge your space for the ritual. Light a candle. Write down your intentions for the next month on a piece of paper. Meditate on your intentions. In a safe place, light the paper on fire to send your intentions into the universe. Then, take a few moments for yourself. Read a book, take a quiet walk, pray, meditate or rest. Take your crystals to bed with you tonight. You can feel the effects of the moon up to a week before and after it occurs.

# NEW MOON  MAY 30TH

The New Moon represents a fresh start and new beginnings.

GOALS FOR THIS MOON CYCLE:

HOW AM I FEELING DURING THIS MOON PHASE?

HOW CAN I EXPERIENCE MORE JOY AND PEACE?

WHAT IN MY LIFE NEEDS NOURISHMENT?

# WAXING CRESCENT      MAY 31ST

The Waxing Crescent Moon Phase represents setting intentions. This moon phase also represents positive changes in your emotional state.

## IN GEMINI

## CRYSTALS FOR THIS MOON

Amethyst - brings inspiration, awakens insight and intuition
Citrine - stimulates the brain, promotes motivation and self-expression
Emerald - supports compassion, trust and forgiveness, opens the heart space
Diopside - offers perspective and boosts creativity, great for manifesting visions

## MOON AFFIRMATION

I believe in myself and have confidence in my abilities. My intentions, hopes, and wishes will be reality because I have the power within me to make it happen.

## MOON RITUAL

This moon is in a growth phase and is an exciting time for positive changes in your life. This moon brings growth, luck and love. Carry a Citrine crystal with you to keep you focused and give you confidence to achieve your goals. Review your goals and keep them where you can see them every day.

# WAXING CRESCENT                    MAY 31ST

INTENTIONS FOR THIS MOON CYCLE:




HOW AM I FEELING DURING THIS MOON PHASE?




WHERE DO I FIND INSPIRATION? WHY?




WHAT IS MY BODY FEELING RIGHT NOW?

# MONTH-END REFLECTION

WHAT GOALS DID I ACHIEVE THIS PAST MONTH?

WHAT ARE SOME THINGS I CAN IMPROVE ON NEXT MONTH?

WHAT ARE THE THREE MOST IMPORTANT THINGS I LEARNED THIS PAST MONTH?

WHAT DO I LOOK FORWARD TO ACHIEVING NEXT MONTH?

# JUNE 2022

1st-6th WAXING CRESCENT
7th FIRST QUARTER
8th-13th WAXING GIBBOUS
14th FULL MOON
15th-20th WANING GIBBOUS
21st LAST QUARTER
22nd-27th WANING CRESCENT
28th NEW MOON
29th-30th WAXING CRESCENT

## SUPERMOON
June 14th

## JUNE SOLSTICE
June 21st

(EST USA Time Zone)

# WAXING CRESCENT       JUN 1ST- 6TH

The Waxing Crescent Moon Phase represents setting intentions. This moon phase also represents positive changes in your emotional state.

1ST- 3RD IN CANCER
4TH- 5TH IN LEO
6TH IN VIRGO

## CRYSTALS FOR THIS MOON

Amethyst - brings inspiration, awakens insight and intuition
Citrine - stimulates the brain, promotes motivation and self-expression
Emerald - supports compassion, trust and forgiveness, opens the heart space
Diopside - offers perspective and boosts creativity, great for manifesting visions

## MOON AFFIRMATION

I believe in myself and have confidence in my abilities. My intentions, hopes, and wishes will be reality because I have the power within me to make it happen.

## MOON RITUAL

This moon is in a growth phase and is an exciting time for positive changes in your life. This moon brings growth, luck and love. Carry a Citrine crystal with you to keep you focused and give you confidence to achieve your goals. Review your goals and keep them where you can see them every day.

# WAXING CRESCENT        JUN 1ST - 6TH

INTENTIONS FOR THIS MOON CYCLE:

HOW AM I FEELING DURING THIS MOON PHASE?

WHERE DO I FIND INSPIRATION? WHY?

WHAT IS MY BODY FEELING RIGHT NOW?

# FIRST QUARTER  JUN 7TH

## MOON IN VIRGO

Now is a time for decision-making. The strong creative energy inside of you will come to the surface today. Some good activities to do include reading, writing, learning, and teaching. This moon phase will bring the ability to be more productive and accomplish tasks that normally take you longer to complete. This will be a very busy time for you, so make sure to take time to relax as well. Focus on the most important tasks first and remember to stay calm and grounded.
If you are a Virgo, you will feel a stronger effect.

## CRYSTALS FOR THIS MOON

Carnelian - great for motivation, courage and inspiration
Blue Lace Agate - a soothing, calming stone for peace
Lapis Lazuli - helps to open the third eye for heightened intuition

## MOON AFFIRMATION

I am taking action to move toward my dreams by using courage and creativity.
I will also remember to take time to care for myself during this cycle.

## MOON RITUAL

Use your Carnelian to create an elixir and sip on it throughout these two days. Place the stone next to a glass of filtered water and leave it by the window to soak up the moon's energy overnight. Say your intentions out loud during this process.

# FIRST QUARTER                    JUN 7ᵀᴴ

The First Quarter Moon represents a period of growth and action.

ACTION ITEMS FOR THIS MOON CYCLE:

HOW AM I FEELING DURING THIS MOON PHASE?

HOW HAVE I BEEN TAKING ACTION TOWARDS MY GOALS?

ARE MY ACTIONS ALIGNED WITH THE INTENTIONS I HAVE SET FOR MYSELF?

# WAXING GIBBOUS — JUN 8TH–13TH

The Waxing Gibbous Moon represents a period of refining and nurturing your goals, hopes and dreams.

8TH–10TH IN LIBRA
11TH–12TH IN SCORPIO
13TH IN SAGITTARIUS

## CRYSTALS FOR THIS MOON

Fluorite - activates all Chakras and helps you to find your divine calling
Citrine - attracts success, prosperity and magic; boosts confidence and mental clarity
Pyrite - helps with motivation and taking action toward goals
Tigers Eye - invites good luck, blocks bad luck and negative energies

## MOON AFFIRMATION

I have planted the seeds that will bring me closer to my hopes and dreams. I let positive thoughts grow in my mind and open my heart to all the good things that are coming my way. I see my goals clearly and I feel them manifesting.

## MOON RITUAL

This is the best time to work on yourself and use this amazing healing energy. Push yourself to do more than usual. This is a good time to refine and improve. Carry Pyrite to keep you motivated and take action before the waning phase begins.

# WAXING GIBBOUS          JUN 8ᵀᴴ- 13ᵀᴴ

INTENTIONS I WANT TO NURTURE DURING
THIS MOON CYCLE:

HOW AM I FEELING DURING THIS MOON PHASE?

WHICH GOALS AM I MOST EXCITED ABOUT?

WHAT IS WORKING FOR ME? WHAT IS NOT?
HOW CAN I IMPROVE?

# FULL STRAWBERRY MOON            JUN 14TH

The Full Moon represents a time to harvest your intentions that have been set and making sure they materialize. The Moon will be located on the opposite side of the Earth as the Sun and its face will be fully illuminated. This full moon was known by early Native American tribes as the Full Strawberry Moon because June is the relatively short season for harvesting strawberries.

## MOON IN SAGITTARIUS

The Full Strawberry Moon in Sagittarius will increase your intuition and cause you to think more about your life than usual. You will really become focused on healing and learning about your true purpose. Pay close attention to your dreams, because messages and thoughts will come to you as you sleep. If you are a Sagittarius, you will feel a stronger effect.

## FULL MOON CRYSTALS

Cleanse your crystals in this Full Moon. Leave them in the moonlight for two nights to clear any absorbed energies. The best crystals to use for this Sagittarius Full Moon are: Aventurine, Azurite, and Clear Quartz. Clear Quartz is also a very powerful crystal to help balance your Chakras during a Full Moon. Set your intentions to find your own personal truth and philosophy of life.

## FULL MOON RITUAL

Smudge sage or diffuse your favorite essential oil to set the tone. Meditate by letting your intuition guide your session. Journal to free your thoughts, follow your heart and pour your thoughts onto the pages. Check in with yourself on your progress toward your goals. Set your intentions and ask the universe to support you in achieving your goals. Feel the power within you!

# FULL MOON                                JUN 14TH

The Full Moon represents a time to harvest your intentions that have been set and making sure they materialize. You can feel the effects of the moon up to a week before and after it occurs.

WHAT EMOTIONS AM I FEELING TODAY?



WHAT DOES MY SOUL NEED?



WHAT HAVE I BEEN NEGLECTING?



WHAT AREAS OF MY LIFE FEEL OUT OF ALIGNMENT?

# WANING GIBBOUS    JUN 15TH-20TH

The Waning Gibbous Moon represents a period of introspection and gratitude. This is also a time to set intentions and declutter your life.

15TH-16TH IN CAPRICORN
17TH-18TH IN AQUARIUS
19TH-20TH IN PISCES

## CRYSTALS FOR THIS MOON

Smoky Quartz - Root Chakra, Grounding
Malachite - Cleanse, Purify, Promote positive energy & gratitude
Blue Calcite - Clears negativity and encourages rest & relaxation
Azurite - Strengthens your intuition and psychic abilities
Unakite Jasper - Opens your heart space and brings energy of love

## MOON AFFIRMATION

I am grounded and able to make good decisions. I will be realistic when setting my intentions and goals. I am filled with gratitude for everything that I have.

## MOON RITUAL

Cleanse your home using Palo Santo or Sage. This will make room for positivity in your life and let go of the negativity. Think about anything you need to let go of in your life. Keep a crystal close while you write a list down on paper and create your action plan to let these things go.

# WANING GIBBOUS          JUN 15TH-20TH

WHAT AM I GRATEFUL FOR?

HOW AM I FEELING DURING THIS MOON PHASE?

HOW CAN I IMPROVE MY MINDFULNESS?

WHAT NEW THINGS HAVE I LEARNED ABOUT MYSELF THIS CYCLE?

# LAST QUARTER       JUN 21ST

## MOON IN ARIES

The moon in Aries can cause you to feel more impulsive, direct and powerful. When combined with a First Quarter moon, you will start taking action. This moon will spark your desires and passions. You will feel a burst of momentum to attack your goals headfirst! Take advantage of this time for great change.

## CRYSTALS FOR THIS MOON

Black Obsidian - Cleanses aura, removes negative energy blockages
Lapis Lazuli - Good for self-awareness and revealing inner truth
Clear Quartz - Helps you move toward your deepest desires in life

## MOON AFFIRMATION

I release all blockages that are preventing me from moving forward in abundance. Negative energy will not hold me back.

## MOON RITUAL

Spend time in nature and work on grounding yourself. Take action and release all negative behaviors. Carry your obsidian to protect you from negativity. Burn or carry Geranium oil with you to rebuild your energy after releasing the negativity.

# LAST QUARTER　　　　　　　　JUN 21ᔆᵀ

The Last (Third) Quarter Moon represents a period of release and self-assessment. Cleanse any mental and physical obstacles through organization and meditation.

WHAT HABITS ARE STOPPING ME FROM REACHING MY GOALS?

HOW AM I FEELING DURING THIS MOON PHASE?

WHAT COULD I HAVE DONE DIFFERENTLY DURING THIS CYCLE?

WHAT AM I HOLDING ON TO THAT NEEDS TO BE RELEASED?

# WANING CRESCENT       JUN 22ND-27TH

The Waning Crescent Moon represents a period of surrender and a time for rest.

22ND IN ARIES
23RD-25TH IN TAURUS
26TH-27TH IN GEMINI

## CRYSTALS FOR THIS MOON

Bloodstone - helps to embrace the transformation you have been through
Rainbow Fluorite - helps to balance emotions during this up and down period
Black Tourmaline - Grounds your spirit, deflects negative energies
Petalite - Brings peace and calm, supports working with Spirit and angel guides
Black Obsidian - Gently grounding and protective, strengthens your aura field

## MOON AFFIRMATION

I remain centered while my emotions change, and I release any emotions I have been repressing. I can remain balanced and take time to care for myself.

## MOON RITUAL

This moon marks the end of the healing cycle. Think of anything you need to do to complete this cycle before the next one begins. Be gentle to yourself and practice some self-care during this time. Do anything that relaxes you and helps you to feel calm and secure. Take a bath with your crystals surrounding you.

# WANING CRESCENT     JUN 22ND-27TH

HOW CAN I IMPROVE MY SELF-CARE?

HOW AM I FEELING DURING THIS MOON PHASE?

WHAT DO I NEED TO DO FOR MYSELF?

IS THERE ANYTHING IN MY LIFE HOLDING ME BACK? HOW CAN I LET GO?

# NEW MOON GUIDE    JUN 28TH

The Moon will be located on the same side of the Earth as the Sun which means you cannot see the moon from Earth.

## MOON IN CANCER

The New Moon in Cancer brings us to a very nurturing and protective place. This moon enhances our dreams and increases intuition. You will start to focus more on what you really want and what you are lacking. You may feel overly needy and overindulgent during this phase as well. Since Cancer is an emotional sign, you may also feel insecure and need to focus on finding a balance between self-love and feelings of inadequacy. Make sure to balance your emotions to limit outbursts on those who are closest to you. If you are a Cancer, you will feel a stronger effect.

## NEW MOON CRYSTALS

Charge your crystals in this new moon. Leave them out for two nights. You cannot see the moon at this time, but the cleansing is still powerful. Crystals that are powerful in the Cancer New Moon are: Carnelian, Peach Moonstone and Smoky Quartz. Set your intentions for patience, confidence and balance.

## NEW MOON RITUAL

Use sage to smudge your space for the ritual. Light a candle. Write down your intentions for the next month on a piece of paper. Meditate on your intentions. In a safe place, light the paper on fire to send your intentions into the universe. Then, take a few moments for yourself. Read a book, take a quiet walk, pray, meditate or rest. Take your crystals to bed with you tonight. You can feel the effects of the moon up to a week before and after it occurs.

# NEW MOON                                   JUN 28TH

The New Moon represents a fresh start and new beginnings.

GOALS FOR THIS MOON CYCLE:

HOW AM I FEELING DURING THIS MOON PHASE?

HOW CAN I EXPERIENCE MORE JOY AND PEACE?

WHAT IN MY LIFE NEEDS NOURISHMENT?

# WAXING CRESCENT  JUN 29TH-30TH

The Waxing Crescent Moon Phase represents setting intentions. This moon phase also represents positive changes in your emotional state.

## IN CANCER

## CRYSTALS FOR THIS MOON

Amethyst - brings inspiration, awakens insight and intuition
Citrine - stimulates the brain, promotes motivation and self-expression
Emerald - supports compassion, trust and forgiveness, opens the heart space
Diopside - offers perspective and boosts creativity, great for manifesting visions

## MOON AFFIRMATION

I believe in myself and have confidence in my abilities. My intentions, hopes, and wishes will be reality because I have the power within me to make it happen.

## MOON RITUAL

This moon is in a growth phase and is an exciting time for positive changes in your life. This moon brings growth, luck and love. Carry a Citrine crystal with you to keep you focused and give you confidence to achieve your goals. Review your goals and keep them where you can see them every day.

# WAXING CRESCENT        JUN 29ᵀᴴ-30ᵀᴴ

INTENTIONS FOR THIS MOON CYCLE:




HOW AM I FEELING DURING THIS MOON PHASE?




WHERE DO I FIND INSPIRATION? WHY?




WHAT IS MY BODY FEELING RIGHT NOW?

# MONTH-END REFLECTION

WHAT GOALS DID I ACHIEVE THIS PAST MONTH?

WHAT ARE SOME THINGS I CAN IMPROVE ON NEXT MONTH?

WHAT ARE THE THREE MOST IMPORTANT THINGS I LEARNED THIS PAST MONTH?

WHAT DO I LOOK FORWARD TO ACHIEVING NEXT MONTH?

# JULY 2022

1st-5th   WAXING CRESCENT
6th-7th   FIRST QUARTER
8th-12th  WAXING GIBBOUS
13th      FULL MOON
14th-19th WANING GIBBOUS
20th      LAST QUARTER
21st-27th WANING CRESCENT
28th      NEW MOON
29th-31st WAXING CRESCENT

SUPERMOON
July 13th

(EST USA Time Zone)

# WAXING CRESCENT  JULY 1ST-5TH

The Waxing Crescent Moon Phase represents setting intentions. This moon phase also represents positive changes in your emotional state.

1ST-2ND IN LEO
3RD-5TH IN VIRGO

## CRYSTALS FOR THIS MOON

Amethyst - brings inspiration, awakens insight and intuition
Citrine - stimulates the brain, promotes motivation and self-expression
Emerald - supports compassion, trust and forgiveness, opens the heart space
Diopside - offers perspective and boosts creativity, great for manifesting visions

## MOON AFFIRMATION

I believe in myself and have confidence in my abilities. My intentions, hopes, and wishes will be reality because I have the power within me to make it happen.

## MOON RITUAL

This moon is in a growth phase and is an exciting time for positive changes in your life. This moon brings growth, luck and love. Carry a Citrine crystal with you to keep you focused and give you confidence to achieve your goals. Review your goals and keep them where you can see them every day.

# WAXING CRESCENT    JULY 1ST-5TH

INTENTIONS FOR THIS MOON CYCLE:

HOW AM I FEELING DURING THIS MOON PHASE?

WHERE DO I FIND INSPIRATION? WHY?

WHAT IS MY BODY FEELING RIGHT NOW?

# FIRST QUARTER          JULY 6TH–7TH

## MOON IN LIBRA

This moon will transform you into an excellent communicator. You will prefer balance and harmony over confrontation. You may find yourself taking longer than usual to make a decision but ultimately you will make the right choice. You may also feel more tired than usual. This is because you may feel more self-critical and suspicious of others. Communicate with yourself, use your crystals to stay grounded and make sure to take plenty of time to relax by meditating and practicing self-care. If you are a Libra, you will feel a stronger effect.

## CRYSTALS FOR THIS MOON

Carnelian - great for motivation, courage and inspiration
Blue Lace Agate - a soothing, calming stone for peace
Lapis Lazuli - helps to open the third eye for heightened intuition

## MOON AFFIRMATION

I am taking action to move toward my dreams by using courage and creativity. I will also remember to take time to care for myself during this cycle.

## MOON RITUAL

Use your Carnelian to create an elixir and sip on it throughout these two days. Place the stone next to a glass of filtered water and leave it by the window to soak up the moon's energy overnight. Say your intentions out loud during this process.

# FIRST QUARTER

JULY 6TH–7TH

The First Quarter Moon represents a period of growth and action.

ACTION ITEMS FOR THIS MOON CYCLE:

HOW AM I FEELING DURING THIS MOON PHASE?

HOW HAVE I BEEN TAKING ACTION TOWARDS MY GOALS?

ARE MY ACTIONS ALIGNED WITH THE INTENTIONS I HAVE SET FOR MYSELF?

# WAXING GIBBOUS      JULY 8TH-12TH

The Waxing Gibbous Moon represents a period of refining and nurturing your goals, hopes and dreams.

8TH-9TH IN SCORPIO
10TH-11TH IN SAGITTARIUS
12TH IN CAPRICORN

## CRYSTALS FOR THIS MOON

Fluorite - activates all Chakras and helps you to find your divine calling
Citrine - attracts success, prosperity and magic; boosts confidence and mental clarity
Pyrite - helps with motivation and taking action toward goals
Tigers Eye - invites good luck, blocks bad luck and negative energies

## MOON AFFIRMATION

I have planted the seeds that will bring me closer to my hopes and dreams. I let positive thoughts grow in my mind and open my heart to all the good things that are coming my way. I see my goals clearly and I feel them manifesting.

## MOON RITUAL

This is the best time to work on yourself and use this amazing healing energy. Push yourself to do more than usual. This is a good time to refine and improve. Carry Pyrite to keep you motivated and take action before the waning phase begins.

# WAXING GIBBOUS JULY 8TH-12TH

INTENTIONS I WANT TO NURTURE DURING
THIS MOON CYCLE:

HOW AM I FEELING DURING THIS MOON PHASE?

WHICH GOALS AM I MOST EXCITED ABOUT?

WHAT IS WORKING FOR ME? WHAT IS NOT?
HOW CAN I IMPROVE?

# FULL BUCK MOON             JULY 13TH

The Full Moon represents a time to harvest your intentions that have been set and making sure they materialize. The Moon will be located on the opposite side of the Earth as the Sun and its face will be fully illuminated. This full moon was known by early Native American tribes as the Full Buck Moon because the male buck deer would begin to grow their new antlers this time of year.

## MOON IN CAPRICORN

The Full Moon in Capricorn will prompt a major spiritual awakening within your soul. The energy will be powerful, and you will feel a strong masculine energy shift. Let go of what is no longer serving your life's purpose and listen to your intuition. This is a great time for transformation. If you are a Capricorn, you will feel a stronger effect.

## FULL MOON CRYSTALS

Cleanse your crystals in this full moon. Leave them in the moonlight for two nights to clear any absorbed energies. The best crystals to use for this Capricorn Full Moon are: Azurite, Citrine, Malachite and Clear Quartz. Clear Quartz is also a very powerful crystal to help balance your Chakras during a Full Moon. Set your intentions to focus on deeper intuition and letting go of what is holding you back.

## FULL MOON RITUAL

Take your crystals outside and place them on the earth. Allow the moon's energy to remove any negative energy that your crystals have been holding. Have a releasing meditation session to let go of bad habits or emotions. Journal about any thoughts that come during this meditation.

# FULL MOON                    JULY 13TH

The Full Moon represents a time to harvest your intentions that have been set and making sure they materialize. You can feel the effects of the moon up to a week before and after it occurs.

## WHAT EMOTIONS AM I FEELING TODAY?

## WHAT DOES MY SOUL NEED?

## WHAT HAVE I BEEN NEGLECTING?

## WHAT AREAS OF MY LIFE FEEL OUT OF ALIGNMENT?

# WANING GIBBOUS        JULY 14TH-19TH

The Waning Gibbous Moon represents a period of introspection and gratitude. This is also a time to set intentions and declutter your life.

14TH-15TH IN AQUARIUS
16TH-17TH IN PISCES
18TH-19TH IN ARIES

## CRYSTALS FOR THIS MOON

Smoky Quartz - Root Chakra, Grounding
Malachite - Cleanse, Purify, Promote positive energy & gratitude
Blue Calcite - Clears negativity and encourages rest & relaxation
Azurite - Strengthens your intuition and psychic abilities
Unakite Jasper - Opens your heart space and brings energy of love

## MOON AFFIRMATION

I am grounded and able to make good decisions. I will be realistic when setting my intentions and goals. I am filled with gratitude for everything that I have.

## MOON RITUAL

Cleanse your home using Palo Santo or Sage. This will make room for positivity in your life and let go of the negativity. Think about anything you need to let go of in your life. Keep a crystal close while you write a list down on paper and create your action plan to let these things go.

# WANING GIBBOUS  JULY 14TH-19TH

WHAT AM I GRATEFUL FOR?




HOW AM I FEELING DURING THIS MOON PHASE?




HOW CAN I IMPROVE MY MINDFULNESS?




WHAT NEW THINGS HAVE I LEARNED ABOUT MYSELF THIS CYCLE?

# LAST QUARTER                                    JULY 20TH

## MOON IN ARIES

The moon in Aries can cause you to feel more impulsive, direct and powerful. When combined with a First Quarter moon, you will start taking action. This moon will spark your desires and passions. You will feel a burst of momentum to attack your goals headfirst! Take advantage of this time for great change.

## CRYSTALS FOR THIS MOON

Black Obsidian - Cleanses aura, removes negative energy blockages
Lapis Lazuli - Good for self-awareness and revealing inner truth
Clear Quartz - Helps you move toward your deepest desires in life

## MOON AFFIRMATION

I release all blockages that are preventing me from moving forward in abundance. Negative energy will not hold me back.

## MOON RITUAL

Spend time in nature and work on grounding yourself. Take action and release all negative behaviors. Carry your obsidian to protect you from negativity. Burn or carry Geranium oil with you to rebuild your energy after releasing the negativity.

# LAST QUARTER                    JULY 20ᵀᴴ

The Last (Third) Quarter Moon represents a period of release and self-assessment. Cleanse any mental and physical obstacles through organization and meditation.

WHAT HABITS ARE STOPPING ME FROM REACHING MY GOALS?

HOW AM I FEELING DURING THIS MOON PHASE?

WHAT COULD I HAVE DONE DIFFERENTLY DURING THIS CYCLE?

WHAT AM I HOLDING ON TO THAT NEEDS TO BE RELEASED?

# WANING CRESCENT    JULY 21ST-27TH

The Waning Crescent Moon represents a period of surrender and a time for rest.

21ST-22ND IN TAURUS
23RD-25TH IN GEMINI
26TH-27TH IN CANCER

## CRYSTALS FOR THIS MOON

Bloodstone - helps to embrace the transformation you have been through
Rainbow Fluorite - helps to balance emotions during this up and down period
Black Tourmaline - Grounds your spirit, deflects negative energies
Petalite - Brings peace and calm, supports working with Spirit and angel guides
Black Obsidian - Gently grounding and protective, strengthens your aura field

## MOON AFFIRMATION

I remain centered while my emotions change, and I release any emotions I have been repressing. I can remain balanced and take time to care for myself.

## MOON RITUAL

This moon marks the end of the healing cycle. Think of anything you need to do to complete this cycle before the next one begins. Be gentle to yourself and practice some self-care during this time. Do anything that relaxes you and helps you to feel calm and secure. Take a bath with your crystals surrounding you.

# WANING CRESCENT  JULY 21ST-27TH

HOW CAN I IMPROVE MY SELF-CARE?




HOW AM I FEELING DURING THIS MOON PHASE?




WHAT DO I NEED TO DO FOR MYSELF?




IS THERE ANYTHING IN MY LIFE HOLDING ME BACK?
HOW CAN I LET GO?

# NEW MOON GUIDE          JULY 28TH

The Moon will be located on the same side of the Earth as the Sun which means you cannot see the moon from Earth.

## MOON IN LEO

The New Moon in Leo will bring greater awareness and self-assurance. You may feel more playful and joyous. Leo brings confidence and the ability to be brave. This moon will push away any feelings of weakness and will have you take huge steps forward in terms of creativity and strength. You will need to go into your own heart and bring out your confidence. Be brave in love and kindness. Create your own path and take huge leaps forward. Set intentions that will energize your own creativity. If you are a Leo, you will feel a stronger effect.

## NEW MOON CRYSTALS

Charge your crystals in this new moon. Leave them out for two nights. You cannot see the moon at this time, but the cleansing is still powerful. Crystals that are powerful in the Leo New Moon are: Ruby, Rhodochrosite, and Sodalite. Set your intentions for strength, confidence and joy.

## NEW MOON RITUAL

Use sage to smudge your space for the ritual. Light a candle. Write down your intentions for the next month on a piece of paper. Meditate on your intentions. In a safe place, light the paper on fire to send your intentions into the universe. Then, take a few moments for yourself. Read a book, take a quiet walk, pray, meditate or rest. Take your crystals to bed with you tonight. You can feel the effects of the moon up to a week before and after it occurs.

# NEW MOON                                    JULY 28TH

The New Moon represents a fresh start and new beginnings.

GOALS FOR THIS MOON CYCLE:




HOW AM I FEELING DURING THIS MOON PHASE?




HOW CAN I EXPERIENCE MORE JOY AND PEACE?




WHAT IN MY LIFE NEEDS NOURISHMENT?

# WAXING CRESCENT      JULY 29TH-31ST

The Waxing Crescent Moon Phase represents setting intentions. This moon phase also represents positive changes in your emotional state.

29TH-30TH IN LEO
31ST IN VIRGO

## CRYSTALS FOR THIS MOON

Amethyst - brings inspiration, awakens insight and intuition
Citrine - stimulates the brain, promotes motivation and self-expression
Emerald - supports compassion, trust and forgiveness, opens the heart space
Diopside - offers perspective and boosts creativity, great for manifesting visions

## MOON AFFIRMATION

I believe in myself and have confidence in my abilities. My intentions, hopes, and wishes will be reality because I have the power within me to make it happen.

## MOON RITUAL

This moon is in a growth phase and is an exciting time for positive changes in your life. This moon brings growth, luck and love. Carry a Citrine crystal with you to keep you focused and give you confidence to achieve your goals. Review your goals and keep them where you can see them every day.

# WAXING CRESCENT      JULY 29TH-31ST

INTENTIONS FOR THIS MOON CYCLE:




HOW AM I FEELING DURING THIS MOON PHASE?




WHERE DO I FIND INSPIRATION? WHY?




WHAT IS MY BODY FEELING RIGHT NOW?

# MONTH-END REFLECTION

WHAT GOALS DID I ACHIEVE THIS PAST MONTH?

WHAT ARE SOME THINGS I CAN IMPROVE ON NEXT MONTH?

WHAT ARE THE THREE MOST IMPORTANT THINGS I LEARNED THIS PAST MONTH?

WHAT DO I LOOK FORWARD TO ACHIEVING NEXT MONTH?

# AUGUST 2022

1st-4th WAXING CRESCENT
5th FIRST QUARTER
6th-10th WAXING GIBBOUS
11th FULL MOON
12th-18th WANING GIBBOUS
19th LAST QUARTER
20th-26th WANING CRESCENT
27th NEW MOON
28th-31st WAXING CRESCENT

SUPERMOON
August 12th

(EST USA Time Zone)

# WAXING CRESCENT             AUG 1ST-4TH

The Waxing Crescent Moon Phase represents setting intentions. This moon phase also represents positive changes in your emotional state.

1ST IN VIRGO
2ND-3RD IN LIBRA
4TH IN SCORPIO

## CRYSTALS FOR THIS MOON

Amethyst - brings inspiration, awakens insight and intuition
Citrine - stimulates the brain, promotes motivation and self-expression
Emerald - supports compassion, trust and forgiveness, opens the heart space
Diopside - offers perspective and boosts creativity, great for manifesting visions

## MOON AFFIRMATION

I believe in myself and have confidence in my abilities. My intentions, hopes, and wishes will be reality because I have the power within me to make it happen.

## MOON RITUAL

This moon is in a growth phase and is an exciting time for positive changes in your life. This moon brings growth, luck and love. Carry a Citrine crystal with you to keep you focused and give you confidence to achieve your goals. Review your goals and keep them where you can see them every day.

# WAXING CRESCENT     AUG 1ST–4TH

INTENTIONS FOR THIS MOON CYCLE:

HOW AM I FEELING DURING THIS MOON PHASE?

WHERE DO I FIND INSPIRATION? WHY?

WHAT IS MY BODY FEELING RIGHT NOW?

# FIRST QUARTER                           AUG 5<sup>TH</sup>

## MOON IN SCORPIO

This moon is going to bring some attitude with it. You may begin to feel more curious, so dig deep, investigate and use this creative energy. Be careful not to be too obsessed, because a Scorpio moon can cause major obsession. You will also feel more focused, sexual and intensely emotional. Make sure to block out any past emotional resentments in order to keep your mood stable. This is a great time to cleanse any past emotional debris, do psychic work, and transform yourself.

## CRYSTALS FOR THIS MOON

Carnelian - great for motivation, courage and inspiration
Blue Lace Agate - a soothing, calming stone for peace
Lapis Lazuli - helps to open the third eye for heightened intuition

## MOON AFFIRMATION

I am taking action to move toward my dreams by using courage and creativity.
I will also remember to take time to care for myself during this cycle.

## MOON RITUAL

Use your Carnelian to create an elixir and sip on it throughout these two days. Place the stone next to a glass of filtered water and leave it by the window to soak up the moon's energy overnight. Say your intentions out loud during this process.

# FIRST QUARTER                             AUG 5ᵀᴴ

The First Quarter Moon represents a period of growth and action.

ACTION ITEMS FOR THIS MOON CYCLE:




HOW AM I FEELING DURING THIS MOON PHASE?




HOW HAVE I BEEN TAKING ACTION TOWARDS MY GOALS?




ARE MY ACTIONS ALIGNED WITH THE INTENTIONS I HAVE SET FOR MYSELF?

# WAXING GIBBOUS         AUG 6TH-10TH

The Waxing Gibbous Moon represents a period of refining and nurturing your goals, hopes and dreams.

6TH IN SCORPIO
7TH-8TH IN SAGITTARIUS
9TH-10TH IN CAPRICORN

## CRYSTALS FOR THIS MOON

Fluorite - activates all Chakras and helps you to find your divine calling
Citrine - attracts success, prosperity and magic; boosts confidence and mental clarity
Pyrite - helps with motivation and taking action toward goals
Tigers Eye - invites good luck, blocks bad luck and negative energies

## MOON AFFIRMATION

I have planted the seeds that will bring me closer to my hopes and dreams. I let positive thoughts grow in my mind and open my heart to all the good things that are coming my way. I see my goals clearly and I feel them manifesting.

## MOON RITUAL

This is the best time to work on yourself and use this amazing healing energy. Push yourself to do more than usual. This is a good time to refine and improve. Carry Pyrite to keep you motivated and take action before the waning phase begins.

# WAXING GIBBOUS      AUG 6TH-10TH

INTENTIONS I WANT TO NURTURE DURING
THIS MOON CYCLE:




HOW AM I FEELING DURING THIS MOON PHASE?




WHICH GOALS AM I MOST EXCITED ABOUT?




WHAT IS WORKING FOR ME? WHAT IS NOT?
HOW CAN I IMPROVE?

# FULL STURGEON MOON            AUG 11TH

The Full Moon represents a time to harvest your intentions that have been set and making sure they materialize. The Moon will be located on the opposite side of the Earth as the Sun and its face will be fully illuminated. This full moon was known by early Native American tribes as the Full Sturgeon Moon because this large fish was most readily caught this time of year.

## MOON IN AQUARIUS

This Full Sturgeon Moon in Aquarius will ask you to put the greater good before yourself and your personal needs, so you need to make sure to not be selfish or hurtful to others. This moon may cause you to question everything including relationships. This is a good time to determine who is worth spending your time and energy on. This is a great moon for embracing change! If you are an Aquarius, you will feel a stronger effect.

## FULL MOON CRYSTALS

Cleanse your crystals in this full moon. Leave them in the moonlight for two nights to clear any absorbed energies. The best crystals to use for this Aquarius Full Moon are: Turquoise, Moldavite, Obsidian, and Sapphire. Clear Quartz is also a very powerful crystal to help balance your Chakras during a Full Moon. Set your intentions to focus on your creativity and potential for change and adventure.

## FULL MOON RITUAL

Sit down and visualize what you wish to do once your goals have been met. Reflect on what you have already accomplished this cycle. Declutter! Make sure everything in your home supports your hopes, wishes and dreams! Clear any clutter in the Southwest area of your home or office space.

# FULL MOON    AUG 11TH

The Full Moon represents a time to harvest your intentions that have been set and making sure they materialize. You can feel the effects of the moon up to a week before and after it occurs.

## WHAT EMOTIONS AM I FEELING TODAY?

## WHAT DOES MY SOUL NEED?

## WHAT HAVE I BEEN NEGLECTING?

## WHAT AREAS OF MY LIFE FEEL OUT OF ALIGNMENT?

# WANING GIBBOUS     AUG 12TH–18TH

The Waning Gibbous Moon represents a period of introspection and gratitude. This is also a time to set intentions and declutter your life.

12TH IN AQUARIUS
13TH–14TH IN PISCES
15TH–16TH IN ARIES
17TH–18TH IN TAURUS

## CRYSTALS FOR THIS MOON

Smoky Quartz – Root Chakra, Grounding
Malachite – Cleanse, Purify, Promote positive energy & gratitude
Blue Calcite – Clears negativity and encourages rest & relaxation
Azurite – Strengthens your intuition and psychic abilities
Unakite Jasper – Opens your heart space and brings energy of love

## MOON AFFIRMATION

I am grounded and able to make good decisions. I will be realistic when setting my intentions and goals. I am filled with gratitude for everything that I have.

## MOON RITUAL

Cleanse your home using Palo Santo or Sage. This will make room for positivity in your life and let go of the negativity. Think about anything you need to let go of in your life. Keep a crystal close while you write a list down on paper and create your action plan to let these things go.

# WANING GIBBOUS         AUG 12TH- 18TH

WHAT AM I GRATEFUL FOR?

HOW AM I FEELING DURING THIS MOON PHASE?

HOW CAN I IMPROVE MY MINDFULNESS?

WHAT NEW THINGS HAVE I LEARNED ABOUT MYSELF THIS CYCLE?

# LAST QUARTER                                    AUG 19TH

### MOON IN GEMINI

This moon is a good time for networking, communicating, and learning. Focus on brainstorming new ideas, meditating, and using expression in writing. You may struggle with concentration right now, so it is best to focus on the highest priorities. Speak to your plants, trim them but avoid planting. Go on a short trip. Take a trip to the library or bookstore. Spend time with your family. Make a list of what you would like to learn that would make your life easier. Keep communications open with others and release yourself from any negative thoughts.

### CRYSTALS FOR THIS MOON

Black Obsidian - Cleanses aura, removes negative energy blockages
Lapis Lazuli - Good for self-awareness and revealing inner truth
Clear Quartz - Helps you move toward your deepest desires in life

### MOON AFFIRMATION

I release all blockages that are preventing me from moving forward in abundance. Negative energy will not hold me back.

### MOON RITUAL

Spend time in nature and work on grounding yourself. Take action and release all negative behaviors. Carry your obsidian to protect you from negativity. Burn or carry Geranium oil with you to rebuild your energy after releasing the negativity.

# LAST QUARTER                             AUG 19TH

The Last (Third) Quarter Moon represents a period of release and self-assessment. Cleanse any mental and physical obstacles through organization and meditation.

WHAT HABITS ARE STOPPING ME FROM REACHING MY GOALS?

HOW AM I FEELING DURING THIS MOON PHASE?

WHAT COULD I HAVE DONE DIFFERENTLY DURING THIS CYCLE?

WHAT AM I HOLDING ON TO THAT NEEDS TO BE RELEASED?

# WANING CRESCENT    AUG 20ᵀᴴ-26ᵀᴴ

The Waning Crescent Moon represents a period of surrender and a time for rest.

20ᵀᴴ-21ˢᵀ IN GEMINI
22ᴺᴰ-23ᴿᴰ IN CANCER
24ᵀᴴ-26ᵀᴴ IN LEO

## CRYSTALS FOR THIS MOON

Bloodstone - helps to embrace the transformation you have been through
Rainbow Fluorite - helps to balance emotions during this up and down period
Black Tourmaline - Grounds your spirit, deflects negative energies
Petalite - Brings peace and calm, supports working with Spirit and angel guides
Black Obsidian - Gently grounding and protective, strengthens your aura field

## MOON AFFIRMATION

I remain centered while my emotions change, and I release any emotions I have been repressing. I can remain balanced and take time to care for myself.

## MOON RITUAL

This moon marks the end of the healing cycle. Think of anything you need to do to complete this cycle before the next one begins. Be gentle to yourself and practice some self-care during this time. Do anything that relaxes you and helps you to feel calm and secure. Take a bath with your crystals surrounding you.

# WANING CRESCENT        AUG 20ᵀᴴ-26ᵀᴴ

HOW CAN I IMPROVE MY SELF-CARE?

HOW AM I FEELING DURING THIS MOON PHASE?

WHAT DO I NEED TO DO FOR MYSELF?

IS THERE ANYTHING IN MY LIFE HOLDING ME BACK?
HOW CAN I LET GO?

# NEW MOON GUIDE          AUG 27TH

The Moon will be located on the same side of the Earth as the Sun which means you cannot see the moon from Earth.

## MOON IN VIRGO

This New Moon in Virgo will assist you with making important changes in your life. This moon will have you wanting to be healthier and more physically fit. This is also a great time to get organized. During this moon, you will be able to get back to your personal goals. This energy will help you to make important life changes. Now is a time to release bad habits, make healthy choices, and learn to live in the present and let go of the past. If you are a Virgo, you will feel a stronger effect.

## NEW MOON CRYSTALS

Charge your crystals in this new moon. Leave them out for two nights. You cannot see the moon at this time, but the cleansing is still powerful.
Crystals that are powerful in the Virgo New Moon are: Magnesite, Lapis Lazuli and Picture Jasper. Set your intentions for emotional balance, self-esteem and motivation for a healthy lifestyle.

## NEW MOON RITUAL

Use sage to smudge your space for the ritual. Light a candle. Write down your intentions for the next month on a piece of paper. Meditate on your intentions. In a safe place, light the paper on fire to send your intentions into the universe. Then, take a few moments for yourself. Read a book, take a quiet walk, pray, meditate or rest. Take your crystals to bed with you tonight. You can feel the effects of the moon up to a week before and after it occurs.

# NEW MOON                           AUG 27TH

The New Moon represents a fresh start and new beginnings.

GOALS FOR THIS MOON CYCLE:




HOW AM I FEELING DURING THIS MOON PHASE?




HOW CAN I EXPERIENCE MORE JOY AND PEACE?




WHAT IN MY LIFE NEEDS NOURISHMENT?

# WAXING CRESCENT    AUG 28TH-31ST

The Waxing Crescent Moon Phase represents setting intentions. This moon phase also represents positive changes in your emotional state.

28TH  IN VIRGO
29TH-31ST  IN LIBRA

## CRYSTALS FOR THIS MOON

Amethyst - brings inspiration, awakens insight and intuition
Citrine - stimulates the brain, promotes motivation and self-expression
Emerald - supports compassion, trust and forgiveness, opens the heart space
Diopside - offers perspective and boosts creativity, great for manifesting visions

## MOON AFFIRMATION

I believe in myself and have confidence in my abilities. My intentions, hopes, and wishes will be reality because I have the power within me to make it happen.

## MOON RITUAL

This moon is in a growth phase and is an exciting time for positive changes in your life. This moon brings growth, luck and love. Carry a Citrine crystal with you to keep you focused and give you confidence to achieve your goals. Review your goals and keep them where you can see them every day.

# WAXING CRESCENT      AUG 28TH–31ST

INTENTIONS FOR THIS MOON CYCLE:

HOW AM I FEELING DURING THIS MOON PHASE?

WHERE DO I FIND INSPIRATION? WHY?

WHAT IS MY BODY FEELING RIGHT NOW?

# MONTH-END REFLECTION

WHAT GOALS DID I ACHIEVE THIS PAST MONTH?

WHAT ARE SOME THINGS I CAN IMPROVE ON NEXT MONTH?

WHAT ARE THE THREE MOST IMPORTANT THINGS I LEARNED THIS PAST MONTH?

WHAT DO I LOOK FORWARD TO ACHIEVING NEXT MONTH?

# SEPTEMBER 2022

1st-2nd WAXING CRESCENT
3rd FIRST QUARTER
4th-9th WAXING GIBBOUS
10th FULL MOON
11th-16th WANING GIBBOUS
17th-18th LAST QUARTER
19th-24th WANING CRESCENT
25th NEW MOON
26th-30th WAXING CRESCENT

## SEPTEMBER EQUINOX
September 23rd

(EST USA Time Zone)

# WAXING CRESCENT        SEPT 1ST-2ND

The Waxing Crescent Moon Phase represents setting intentions. This moon phase also represents positive changes in your emotional state.

## 1ST-2ND IN SCORPIO

### CRYSTALS FOR THIS MOON

Amethyst - brings inspiration, awakens insight and intuition
Citrine - stimulates the brain, promotes motivation and self-expression
Emerald - supports compassion, trust and forgiveness, opens the heart space
Diopside - offers perspective and boosts creativity, great for manifesting visions

### MOON AFFIRMATION

I believe in myself and have confidence in my abilities. My intentions, hopes, and wishes will be reality because I have the power within me to make it happen.

### MOON RITUAL

This moon is in a growth phase and is an exciting time for positive changes in your life. This moon brings growth, luck and love. Carry a Citrine crystal with you to keep you focused and give you confidence to achieve your goals. Review your goals and keep them where you can see them every day.

# WAXING CRESCENT         SEPT 1ST-2ND

INTENTIONS FOR THIS MOON CYCLE:

HOW AM I FEELING DURING THIS MOON PHASE?

WHERE DO I FIND INSPIRATION? WHY?

WHAT IS MY BODY FEELING RIGHT NOW?

# FIRST QUARTER                    SEPT 3ᴿᴰ

## MOON IN SAGITTARIUS

This moon brings an active spirit. You will have an open mind, soul, and attitude and won't be able to sit still. Sagittarius brings the need to explore and explore our curiosities. You will feel the need to travel, study new things, be spontaneous, and spend time with new people in new places. This is the best time to work on any legal matters, travel, and discover hidden truths. Take a new class to explore your abilities or simply use this moon's energy to open your mind further.

## CRYSTALS FOR THIS MOON

Carnelian - great for motivation, courage and inspiration
Blue Lace Agate - a soothing, calming stone for peace
Lapis Lazuli - helps to open the third eye for heightened intuition

## MOON AFFIRMATION

I am taking action to move toward my dreams by using courage and creativity. I will also remember to take time to care for myself during this cycle.

## MOON RITUAL

Use your Carnelian to create an elixir and sip on it throughout these two days. Place the stone next to a glass of filtered water and leave it by the window to soak up the moon's energy overnight. Say your intentions out loud during this process.

# FIRST QUARTER

SEPT 3ᴿᴰ

The First Quarter Moon represents a period of growth and action.

ACTION ITEMS FOR THIS MOON CYCLE:

HOW AM I FEELING DURING THIS MOON PHASE?

HOW HAVE I BEEN TAKING ACTION TOWARDS MY GOALS?

ARE MY ACTIONS ALIGNED WITH THE INTENTIONS I HAVE SET FOR MYSELF?

# WAXING GIBBOUS        SEPT 4TH-9TH

The Waxing Gibbous Moon represents a period of refining and nurturing your goals, hopes and dreams.

4TH IN SAGITTARIUS
5TH-6TH IN CAPRICORN
7TH-8TH IN AQUARIUS
9TH IN PISCES

## CRYSTALS FOR THIS MOON

Fluorite - activates all Chakras and helps you to find your divine calling
Citrine - attracts success, prosperity and magic; boosts confidence and mental clarity
Pyrite - helps with motivation and taking action toward goals
Tigers Eye - invites good luck, blocks bad luck and negative energies

## MOON AFFIRMATION

I have planted the seeds that will bring me closer to my hopes and dreams. I let positive thoughts grow in my mind and open my heart to all the good things that are coming my way. I see my goals clearly and I feel them manifesting.

## MOON RITUAL

This is the best time to work on yourself and use this amazing healing energy. Push yourself to do more than usual. This is a good time to refine and improve. Carry Pyrite to keep you motivated and take action before the waning phase begins.

# WAXING GIBBOUS

**SEPT 4TH - 9TH**

INTENTIONS I WANT TO NURTURE DURING THIS MOON CYCLE:




HOW AM I FEELING DURING THIS MOON PHASE?




WHICH GOALS AM I MOST EXCITED ABOUT?




WHAT IS WORKING FOR ME? WHAT IS NOT? HOW CAN I IMPROVE?

# FULL CORN MOON          SEPT 10TH

The Full Moon represents a time to harvest your intentions that have been set and making sure they materialize. The Moon will be located on the opposite side of the Earth as the Sun and its face will be fully illuminated. This full moon was known by early Native American tribes as the Full Corn Moon because this marked the time of year when corn was harvested.

## MOON IN PISCES

The Full Moon in Pisces will have you seeing things with a higher meaning. You will become more aware that you are just one small piece of the giant puzzle of the universe. You should work to find meanings in your relationships and all things around you. This moon is great for clairvoyance, telepathy, music and art. This is a great time to recharge your spirit, be centered and stay calm.
If you are a Pisces, you will feel a stronger effect.

## FULL MOON CRYSTALS

Cleanse your crystals in this full moon. Leave them in the moonlight for two nights to clear any absorbed energies. The best crystals to use for this Pisces Full Moon are: Amethyst, Smoky Quartz, Rose Quartz, and Sapphire. Clear Quartz is also a very powerful crystal to help balance your Chakras during a Full Moon. Set your intentions to focus on your emotions, intuition and compassion.

## FULL MOON RITUAL

Fill a pitcher with water and leave it out overnight in the moonlight. Bring the water inside the next day and use it to cleanse your crystals, wash your face, or anything else you need it for. Write your wishes with a pen and burn them in a candle flame under the moon. Do a Full Moon meditation session.

# FULL MOON                           SEPT 10TH

The Full Moon represents a time to harvest your intentions that have been set and making sure they materialize. You can feel the effects of the moon up to a week before and after it occurs.

## WHAT EMOTIONS AM I FEELING TODAY?

## WHAT DOES MY SOUL NEED?

## WHAT HAVE I BEEN NEGLECTING?

## WHAT AREAS OF MY LIFE FEEL OUT OF ALIGNMENT?

# WANING GIBBOUS      SEPT 11TH-16TH

The Waning Gibbous Moon represents a period of introspection and gratitude. This is also a time to set intentions and declutter your life.

11TH-12TH IN ARIES
13TH-15TH IN TAURUS
16TH IN GEMINI

## CRYSTALS FOR THIS MOON

Smoky Quartz - Root Chakra, Grounding
Malachite - Cleanse, Purify, Promote positive energy & gratitude
Blue Calcite - Clears negativity and encourages rest & relaxation
Azurite - Strengthens your intuition and psychic abilities
Unakite Jasper - Opens your heart space and brings energy of love

## MOON AFFIRMATION

I am grounded and able to make good decisions. I will be realistic when setting my intentions and goals. I am filled with gratitude for everything that I have.

## MOON RITUAL

Cleanse your home using Palo Santo or Sage. This will make room for positivity in your life and let go of the negativity. Think about anything you need to let go of in your life. Keep a crystal close while you write a list down on paper and create your action plan to let these things go.

# WANING GIBBOUS      SEPT 11ᵀᴴ-16ᵀᴴ

WHAT AM I GRATEFUL FOR?

HOW AM I FEELING DURING THIS MOON PHASE?

HOW CAN I IMPROVE MY MINDFULNESS?

WHAT NEW THINGS HAVE I LEARNED ABOUT MYSELF THIS CYCLE?

# LAST QUARTER      SEPT 17TH–18TH

### 17TH IN GEMINI
This phase in Gemini is great for networking, bringing people together, sharing information and learning. Just make sure to try to stay focused even with everything going on around you.

### 18TH IN CANCER
Today you will feel the need for quite time, safety and comfort at home. Stay in, relax and do something for yourself. This is a very healing moon energy.

### CRYSTALS FOR THIS MOON
Black Obsidian - Cleanses aura, removes negative energy blockages
Lapis Lazuli - Good for self-awareness and revealing inner truth
Clear Quartz - Helps you move toward your deepest desires in life

### MOON AFFIRMATION
I release all blockages that are preventing me from moving forward in abundance. Negative energy will not hold me back.

### MOON RITUAL
Spend time in nature and work on grounding yourself. Take action and release all negative behaviors. Carry your obsidian to protect you from negativity. Burn or carry Geranium oil with you to rebuild your energy after releasing the negativity.

# LAST QUARTER            SEPT 17ᵀᴴ-18ᵀᴴ

The Last (Third) Quarter Moon represents a period of release and self-assessment. Cleanse any mental and physical obstacles through organization and meditation.

WHAT HABITS ARE STOPPING ME FROM REACHING MY GOALS?

HOW AM I FEELING DURING THIS MOON PHASE?

WHAT COULD I HAVE DONE DIFFERENTLY DURING THIS CYCLE?

WHAT AM I HOLDING ON TO THAT NEEDS TO BE RELEASED?

# WANING CRESCENT        SEPT 19TH-24TH

The Waning Crescent Moon represents a period of surrender and a time for rest.

19TH-20TH IN CANCER
21ST-22ND IN LEO
23RD-24TH IN VIRGO

## CRYSTALS FOR THIS MOON

Bloodstone - helps to embrace the transformation you have been through
Rainbow Fluorite - helps to balance emotions during this up and down period
Black Tourmaline - Grounds your spirit, deflects negative energies
Petalite - Brings peace and calm, supports working with Spirit and angel guides
Black Obsidian - Gently grounding and protective, strengthens your aura field

## MOON AFFIRMATION

I remain centered while my emotions change, and I release any emotions I have been repressing. I can remain balanced and take time to care for myself.

## MOON RITUAL

This moon marks the end of the healing cycle. Think of anything you need to do to complete this cycle before the next one begins. Be gentle to yourself and practice some self-care during this time. Do anything that relaxes you and helps you to feel calm and secure. Take a bath with your crystals surrounding you.

# WANING CRESCENT      SEPT 19TH-24TH

HOW CAN I IMPROVE MY SELF-CARE?

HOW AM I FEELING DURING THIS MOON PHASE?

WHAT DO I NEED TO DO FOR MYSELF?

IS THERE ANYTHING IN MY LIFE HOLDING ME BACK? HOW CAN I LET GO?

# NEW MOON GUIDE — SEPT 25TH

The Moon will be located on the same side of the Earth as the Sun which means you cannot see the moon from Earth.

## MOON IN VIRGO

This New Moon in Virgo will assist you with making important changes in your life. This moon will have you wanting to be healthier and more physically fit. This is also a great time to get organized. During this moon, you will be able to get back to your personal goals. This energy will help you to make important life changes. Now is a time to release bad habits, make healthy choices, and learn to live in the present and let go of the past. If you are a Virgo, you will feel a stronger effect.

## NEW MOON CRYSTALS

Charge your crystals in this new moon. Leave them out for two nights. You cannot see the moon at this time, but the cleansing is still powerful. Crystals that are powerful in the Virgo New Moon are: Magnesite, Lapis Lazuli and Picture Jasper. Set your intentions for emotional balance, self-esteem and motivation for a healthy lifestyle.

## NEW MOON RITUAL

Use sage to smudge your space for the ritual. Light a candle. Write down your intentions for the next month on a piece of paper. Meditate on your intentions. In a safe place, light the paper on fire to send your intentions into the universe. Then, take a few moments for yourself. Read a book, take a quiet walk, pray, meditate or rest. Take your crystals to bed with you tonight. You can feel the effects of the moon up to a week before and after it occurs.

# NEW MOON                    SEPT 25TH

The New Moon represents a fresh start and new beginnings.

GOALS FOR THIS MOON CYCLE:




HOW AM I FEELING DURING THIS MOON PHASE?




HOW CAN I EXPERIENCE MORE JOY AND PEACE?




WHAT IN MY LIFE NEEDS NOURISHMENT?

# WAXING CRESCENT          SEPT 26TH-30TH

The Waxing Crescent Moon Phase represents setting intentions. This moon phase also represents positive changes in your emotional state.

26TH-27TH IN LIBRA
28TH-29TH IN SCORPIO
30TH IN SAGITTARIUS

## CRYSTALS FOR THIS MOON

Amethyst - brings inspiration, awakens insight and intuition
Citrine - stimulates the brain, promotes motivation and self-expression
Emerald - supports compassion, trust and forgiveness, opens the heart space
Diopside - offers perspective and boosts creativity, great for manifesting visions

## MOON AFFIRMATION

I believe in myself and have confidence in my abilities. My intentions, hopes, and wishes will be reality because I have the power within me to make it happen.

## MOON RITUAL

This moon is in a growth phase and is an exciting time for positive changes in your life. This moon brings growth, luck and love. Carry a Citrine crystal with you to keep you focused and give you confidence to achieve your goals. Review your goals and keep them where you can see them every day.

# WAXING CRESCENT        SEPT 26ᵀᴴ - 30ᵀᴴ

INTENTIONS FOR THIS MOON CYCLE:

HOW AM I FEELING DURING THIS MOON PHASE?

WHERE DO I FIND INSPIRATION? WHY?

WHAT IS MY BODY FEELING RIGHT NOW?

# MONTH-END REFLECTION

WHAT GOALS DID I ACHIEVE THIS PAST MONTH?

WHAT ARE SOME THINGS I CAN IMPROVE ON NEXT MONTH?

WHAT ARE THE THREE MOST IMPORTANT THINGS I LEARNED THIS PAST MONTH?

WHAT DO I LOOK FORWARD TO ACHIEVING NEXT MONTH?

# OCTOBER 2022

1st WAXING CRESCENT
2nd-3rd FIRST QUARTER
4th-8th WAXING GIBBOUS
9th FULL MOON
10th-16th WANING GIBBOUS
17th LAST QUARTER
18th-24th WANING CRESCENT
25th NEW MOON
26th-31st WAXING CRESCENT

PARTIAL SOLAR ECLIPSE
October 25th

(EST USA Time Zone)

# WAXING CRESCENT      OCT 1ST

The Waxing Crescent Moon Phase represents setting intentions. This moon phase also represents positive changes in your emotional state.

## IN SAGITTARIUS

## CRYSTALS FOR THIS MOON

Amethyst - brings inspiration, awakens insight and intuition
Citrine - stimulates the brain, promotes motivation and self-expression
Emerald - supports compassion, trust and forgiveness, opens the heart space
Diopside - offers perspective and boosts creativity, great for manifesting visions

## MOON AFFIRMATION

I believe in myself and have confidence in my abilities. My intentions, hopes, and wishes will be reality because I have the power within me to make it happen.

## MOON RITUAL

This moon is in a growth phase and is an exciting time for positive changes in your life. This moon brings growth, luck and love. Carry a Citrine crystal with you to keep you focused and give you confidence to achieve your goals. Review your goals and keep them where you can see them every day.

# WAXING CRESCENT                OCT 1ST

INTENTIONS FOR THIS MOON CYCLE:

HOW AM I FEELING DURING THIS MOON PHASE?

WHERE DO I FIND INSPIRATION? WHY?

WHAT IS MY BODY FEELING RIGHT NOW?

# FIRST QUARTER     OCT 2ND–3RD

### MOON IN CAPRICORN

When the moon is in Capricorn, you will feel more productive and serious about most things. This is because Capricorn is an Earth sign and this sign craves substance. With the extra patience and discipline this moon brings, you should focus on overcoming any difficult obstacles, finalizing business plans, and manifesting your goals. Your ambitious side will feel more intense and now is the best time to dig deep and make sure you are ready to achieve your goals.

### CRYSTALS FOR THIS MOON

Carnelian - great for motivation, courage and inspiration
Blue Lace Agate - a soothing, calming stone for peace
Lapis Lazuli - helps to open the third eye for heightened intuition

### MOON AFFIRMATION

I am taking action to move toward my dreams by using courage and creativity.
I will also remember to take time to care for myself during this cycle.

### MOON RITUAL

Use your Carnelian to create an elixir and sip on it throughout these two days. Place the stone next to a glass of filtered water and leave it by the window to soak up the moon's energy overnight. Say your intentions out loud during this process.

# FIRST QUARTER         OCT 2^(ND) - 3^(RD)

The First Quarter Moon represents a period of growth and action.

ACTION ITEMS FOR THIS MOON CYCLE:

HOW AM I FEELING DURING THIS MOON PHASE?

HOW HAVE I BEEN TAKING ACTION TOWARDS MY GOALS?

ARE MY ACTIONS ALIGNED WITH THE INTENTIONS I HAVE SET FOR MYSELF?

# WAXING GIBBOUS  OCT 4ᵀᴴ-8ᵀᴴ

The Waxing Gibbous Moon represents a period of refining and nurturing your goals, hopes and dreams.

4ᵀᴴ-5ᵀᴴ IN AQUARIUS
6ᵀᴴ-7ᵀᴴ IN PISCES
8ᵀᴴ IN ARIES

## CRYSTALS FOR THIS MOON

Fluorite - activates all Chakras and helps you to find your divine calling
Citrine - attracts success, prosperity and magic; boosts confidence and mental clarity
Pyrite - helps with motivation and taking action toward goals
Tigers Eye - invites good luck, blocks bad luck and negative energies

## MOON AFFIRMATION

I have planted the seeds that will bring me closer to my hopes and dreams. I let positive thoughts grow in my mind and open my heart to all the good things that are coming my way. I see my goals clearly and I feel them manifesting.

## MOON RITUAL

This is the best time to work on yourself and use this amazing healing energy. Push yourself to do more than usual. This is a good time to refine and improve. Carry Pyrite to keep you motivated and take action before the waning phase begins.

# WAXING GIBBOUS    OCT 4ᵀᴴ-8ᵀᴴ

INTENTIONS I WANT TO NURTURE DURING
THIS MOON CYCLE:




HOW AM I FEELING DURING THIS MOON PHASE?




WHICH GOALS AM I MOST EXCITED ABOUT?




WHAT IS WORKING FOR ME? WHAT IS NOT?
HOW CAN I IMPROVE?

# FULL HUNTERS MOON                    OCT 9TH

The Full Moon represents a time to harvest your intentions that have been set and making sure they materialize. The Moon will be located on the opposite side of the Earth as the Sun and its face will be fully illuminated. This full moon was known by early Native American tribes as the Full Hunters Moon because this is the time of year that is best to start hunting.

## MOON IN ARIES

The Full Moon in Aries will cause your energy to be more direct, daring and independent. Start planting seeds for new beginnings, plan new career goals and take action on new ideas. Be bold, self-expressive and stand up for yourself. If you are an Aries, you will feel a stronger effect.

## FULL MOON CRYSTALS

Cleanse your crystals in this full moon. Leave them in the moonlight for two nights to clear any absorbed energies. The best crystals to use for this Aries Full Moon are: Carnelian, Malachite, Citrine and Bloodstone. Clear Quartz is also a very powerful crystal to help balance your Chakras during a Full Moon. Set your intentions to bring courage, adjust your goals, get confidence and move forward from the past.

## FULL MOON RITUAL

Grab a darker stone such as onyx, hematite or obsidian. Smudge yourself and your space in either sage or palo santo. Sit down in a quiet place and focus on your breathing. Take this moment to acknowledge what is beautiful in your life and affirm that you are fully invested in making your life better.

# FULL MOON                           OCT 9TH

The Full Moon represents a time to harvest your intentions that have been set and making sure they materialize. You can feel the effects of the moon up to a week before and after it occurs.

WHAT EMOTIONS AM I FEELING TODAY?




WHAT DOES MY SOUL NEED?




WHAT HAVE I BEEN NEGLECTING?




WHAT AREAS OF MY LIFE FEEL OUT OF ALIGNMENT?

# WANING GIBBOUS          OCT 10TH-16TH

The Waning Gibbous Moon represents a period of introspection and gratitude. This is also a time to set intentions and declutter your life.

10TH IN ARIES
11TH-12TH IN TAURUS
13TH-15TH IN GEMINI
16TH IN CANCER

## CRYSTALS FOR THIS MOON

Smoky Quartz - Root Chakra, Grounding
Malachite - Cleanse, Purify, Promote positive energy & gratitude
Blue Calcite - Clears negativity and encourages rest & relaxation
Azurite - Strengthens your intuition and psychic abilities
Unakite Jasper - Opens your heart space and brings energy of love

## MOON AFFIRMATION

I am grounded and able to make good decisions. I will be realistic when setting my intentions and goals. I am filled with gratitude for everything that I have.

## MOON RITUAL

Cleanse your home using Palo Santo or Sage. This will make room for positivity in your life and let go of the negativity. Think about anything you need to let go of in your life. Keep a crystal close while you write a list down on paper and create your action plan to let these things go.

# WANING GIBBOUS         OCT 10TH-16TH

WHAT AM I GRATEFUL FOR?




HOW AM I FEELING DURING THIS MOON PHASE?




HOW CAN I IMPROVE MY MINDFULNESS?




WHAT NEW THINGS HAVE I LEARNED ABOUT MYSELF THIS CYCLE?

# LAST QUARTER  OCT 17ᵀᴴ

## MOON IN CANCER

This Cancer moon will pull you toward family and you will feel a strong urge to nurture and care for those around you. Now is a time to be surrounded by your loved ones. This moon also brings out kindness and you may spend more time helping others. Use this time to express yourself, perform random acts of kindness, and journal. If you are Cancer, you will feel a stronger effect.

## CRYSTALS FOR THIS MOON

Black Obsidian - Cleanses aura, removes negative energy blockages
Lapis Lazuli - Good for self-awareness and revealing inner truth
Clear Quartz - Helps you move toward your deepest desires in life

## MOON AFFIRMATION

I release all blockages that are preventing me from moving forward in abundance. Negative energy will not hold me back.

## MOON RITUAL

Spend time in nature and work on grounding yourself. Take action and release all negative behaviors. Carry your obsidian to protect you from negativity. Burn or carry Geranium oil with you to rebuild your energy after releasing the negativity.

# LAST QUARTER                OCT 17ᵀᴴ

The Last (Third) Quarter Moon represents a period of release and self-assessment. Cleanse any mental and physical obstacles through organization and meditation.

WHAT HABITS ARE STOPPING ME FROM REACHING MY GOALS?


HOW AM I FEELING DURING THIS MOON PHASE?


WHAT COULD I HAVE DONE DIFFERENTLY DURING THIS CYCLE?


WHAT AM I HOLDING ON TO THAT NEEDS TO BE RELEASED?

# WANING CRESCENT          OCT 18TH-24TH

The Waning Crescent Moon represents a period of surrender and a time for rest.

18TH-20TH IN LEO
21ST-22ND IN VIRGO
23RD-24TH IN LIBRA

## CRYSTALS FOR THIS MOON

Bloodstone - helps to embrace the transformation you have been through
Rainbow Fluorite - helps to balance emotions during this up and down period
Black Tourmaline - Grounds your spirit, deflects negative energies
Petalite - Brings peace and calm, supports working with Spirit and angel guides
Black Obsidian - Gently grounding and protective, strengthens your aura field

## MOON AFFIRMATION

I remain centered while my emotions change, and I release any emotions I have been repressing. I can remain balanced and take time to care for myself.

## MOON RITUAL

This moon marks the end of the healing cycle. Think of anything you need to do to complete this cycle before the next one begins. Be gentle to yourself and practice some self-care during this time. Do anything that relaxes you and helps you to feel calm and secure. Take a bath with your crystals surrounding you.

# WANING CRESCENT        OCT 18ᵀᴴ-24ᵀᴴ

HOW CAN I IMPROVE MY SELF-CARE?




HOW AM I FEELING DURING THIS MOON PHASE?




WHAT DO I NEED TO DO FOR MYSELF?




IS THERE ANYTHING IN MY LIFE HOLDING ME BACK?
HOW CAN I LET GO?

# NEW MOON GUIDE  OCT 25TH

The Moon will be located on the same side of the Earth as the Sun which means you cannot see the moon from Earth.

## MOON IN SCORPIO

The New Moon in Scorpio offers a new opportunity to look within yourself and healing any darkness in your soul. Focus on letting emotions out and work hard on healing during this time. Face your inner demons and embrace the new life ahead. Now is a good time to pamper yourself by taking a long bath, meditating on your inner power and planting the seeds to your inner desires. If you are a Scorpio, you will feel a stronger effect.

## NEW MOON CRYSTALS

Charge your crystals in this new moon. Leave them out for two nights. You cannot see the moon at this time, but the cleansing is still powerful. Crystals that are powerful in the Scorpio New Moon are: Green Aventurine, Rutilated Quartz and Smoky Quartz. Set your intentions for self-improvement, renewed energy and releasing what you have been holding in your heart.

## NEW MOON RITUAL

Use sage to smudge your space for the ritual. Light a candle. Write down your intentions for the next month on a piece of paper. Meditate on your intentions. In a safe place, light the paper on fire to send your intentions into the universe. Then, take a few moments for yourself. Read a book, take a quiet walk, pray, meditate or rest. Take your crystals to bed with you tonight. You can feel the effects of the moon up to a week before and after it occurs.

# NEW MOON                               OCT 25TH

The New Moon represents a fresh start and new beginnings.

GOALS FOR THIS MOON CYCLE:




HOW AM I FEELING DURING THIS MOON PHASE?




HOW CAN I EXPERIENCE MORE JOY AND PEACE?




WHAT IN MY LIFE NEEDS NOURISHMENT?

# WAXING CRESCENT  OCT 26TH–31ST

The Waxing Crescent Moon Phase represents setting intentions. This moon phase also represents positive changes in your emotional state.

26TH IN SCORPIO
27TH–28TH IN SAGITTARIUS
29TH–30TH IN CAPRICORN
31ST IN AQUARIUS

## CRYSTALS FOR THIS MOON

Amethyst – brings inspiration, awakens insight and intuition
Citrine – stimulates the brain, promotes motivation and self-expression
Emerald – supports compassion, trust and forgiveness, opens the heart space
Diopside – offers perspective and boosts creativity, great for manifesting visions

## MOON AFFIRMATION

I believe in myself and have confidence in my abilities. My intentions, hopes, and wishes will be reality because I have the power within me to make it happen.

## MOON RITUAL

This moon is in a growth phase and is an exciting time for positive changes in your life. This moon brings growth, luck and love. Carry a Citrine crystal with you to keep you focused and give you confidence to achieve your goals. Review your goals and keep them where you can see them every day.

# WAXING CRESCENT     OCT 26TH–31ST

INTENTIONS FOR THIS MOON CYCLE:

HOW AM I FEELING DURING THIS MOON PHASE?

WHERE DO I FIND INSPIRATION? WHY?

WHAT IS MY BODY FEELING RIGHT NOW?

# MONTH-END REFLECTION

WHAT GOALS DID I ACHIEVE THIS PAST MONTH?

WHAT ARE SOME THINGS I CAN IMPROVE ON NEXT MONTH?

WHAT ARE THE THREE MOST IMPORTANT THINGS I LEARNED THIS PAST MONTH?

WHAT DO I LOOK FORWARD TO ACHIEVING NEXT MONTH?

# NOVEMBER 2022

1st — FIRST QUARTER
2nd-7th — WAXING GIBBOUS
8th — FULL MOON
9th-15th — WANING GIBBOUS
16th — LAST QUARTER
17th-22nd — WANING CRESCENT
23rd — NEW MOON
24th-29th — WAXING CRESCENT
30th — FIRST QUARTER

**TOTAL LUNAR ECLIPSE**
November 8th

(EST USA Time Zone)

# FIRST QUARTER                NOV 1ˢᵀ

## MOON IN AQUARIUS

This moon in Aquarius will bring you out of your comfort zone by convincing you to accept sudden changes of plans or going to an unexpected event. This is a rebellious, impulsive moon! This is a great time for alternative therapies such as energy healing, Reiki, acupuncture, or group gatherings. Free your mind by trying Aquarius Yoga. In meditation, focus on your root chakra to keep you grounded and focused.

## CRYSTALS FOR THIS MOON

Carnelian - great for motivation, courage and inspiration
Blue Lace Agate - a soothing, calming stone for peace
Lapis Lazuli - helps to open the third eye for heightened intuition

## MOON AFFIRMATION

I am taking action to move toward my dreams by using courage and creativity.
I will also remember to take time to care for myself during this cycle.

## MOON RITUAL

Use your Carnelian to create an elixir and sip on it throughout these two days. Place the stone next to a glass of filtered water and leave it by the window to soak up the moon's energy overnight. Say your intentions out loud during this process.

# FIRST QUARTER                                NOV 1ST

The First Quarter Moon represents a period of growth and action.

ACTION ITEMS FOR THIS MOON CYCLE:

HOW AM I FEELING DURING THIS MOON PHASE?

HOW HAVE I BEEN TAKING ACTION TOWARDS MY GOALS?

ARE MY ACTIONS ALIGNED WITH THE INTENTIONS I HAVE SET FOR MYSELF?

# WAXING GIBBOUS          NOV 2ND - 7TH

The Waxing Gibbous Moon represents a period of refining and nurturing your goals, hopes and dreams.

2ND IN AQUARIUS
3RD - 4TH IN PISCES
5TH - 6TH IN ARIES
7TH IN TAURUS

## CRYSTALS FOR THIS MOON

Fluorite - activates all Chakras and helps you to find your divine calling
Citrine - attracts success, prosperity and magic; boosts confidence and mental clarity
Pyrite - helps with motivation and taking action toward goals
Tigers Eye - invites good luck, blocks bad luck and negative energies

## MOON AFFIRMATION

I have planted the seeds that will bring me closer to my hopes and dreams. I let positive thoughts grow in my mind and open my heart to all the good things that are coming my way. I see my goals clearly and I feel them manifesting.

## MOON RITUAL

This is the best time to work on yourself and use this amazing healing energy. Push yourself to do more than usual. This is a good time to refine and improve. Carry Pyrite to keep you motivated and take action before the waning phase begins.

# WAXING GIBBOUS      NOV 2ND - 7TH

INTENTIONS I WANT TO NURTURE DURING
THIS MOON CYCLE:




HOW AM I FEELING DURING THIS MOON PHASE?




WHICH GOALS AM I MOST EXCITED ABOUT?




WHAT IS WORKING FOR ME? WHAT IS NOT?
HOW CAN I IMPROVE?

# FULL BEAVER MOON         NOV 8TH

The Full Moon represents a time to harvest your intentions that have been set and making sure they materialize. The Moon will be located on the opposite side of the Earth as the Sun and its face will be fully illuminated. This full moon was known by early Native American tribes as the Full Beaver Moon because this was the time of year to set beaver traps before the water froze.

## MOON IN TAURUS

The Full Moon in Taurus has dynamic energy. This is a great time to get things done. This moon can deliver powerful results if you put in the effort. It also represents a rare opportunity to fully express yourself. This energy is great for peace, growth, and money. Focus on making a list of things you want to accomplish this cycle. If you are a Taurus, you will feel a stronger effect.

## FULL MOON CRYSTALS

Cleanse your crystals in this full moon. Leave them in the moonlight for two nights to clear any absorbed energies. The best crystals to use for this Taurus Full Moon are: Lapis Lazuli, Celestite, Blue Quartz and Labradorite. Clear Quartz is also a very powerful crystal to help balance your Chakras during a Full Moon. Set your intentions to open your throat chakra, expand self expression and creativity and focus on your intuition.

## FULL MOON RITUAL

Soak up some beauty with a moon goddess bath. Add Epsom salt, Himalayan pink salt, your favorite essential oil, and your favorite dried flowers or fresh flower petals. Bring a rose quartz with you. Relax and embrace all of the emotions that come to you during this bath time. Journal your thoughts.

# FULL MOON                    NOV 8TH

The Full Moon represents a time to harvest your intentions that have been set and making sure they materialize. You can feel the effects of the moon up to a week before and after it occurs.

## WHAT EMOTIONS AM I FEELING TODAY?

## WHAT DOES MY SOUL NEED?

## WHAT HAVE I BEEN NEGLECTING?

## WHAT AREAS OF MY LIFE FEEL OUT OF ALIGNMENT?

# WANING GIBBOUS       NOV 9TH-15TH

The Waning Gibbous Moon represents a period of introspection and gratitude. This is also a time to set intentions and declutter your life.

9TH-11TH IN GEMINI
12TH-13TH IN CANCER
14TH-15TH IN LEO

## CRYSTALS FOR THIS MOON
Smoky Quartz - Root Chakra, Grounding
Malachite - Cleanse, Purify, Promote positive energy & gratitude
Blue Calcite - Clears negativity and encourages rest & relaxation
Azurite - Strengthens your intuition and psychic abilities
Unakite Jasper - Opens your heart space and brings energy of love

## MOON AFFIRMATION
I am grounded and able to make good decisions. I will be realistic when setting my intentions and goals. I am filled with gratitude for everything that I have.

## MOON RITUAL
Cleanse your home using Palo Santo or Sage. This will make room for positivity in your life and let go of the negativity. Think about anything you need to let go of in your life. Keep a crystal close while you write a list down on paper and create your action plan to let these things go.

# WANING GIBBOUS    NOV 9TH – 15TH

WHAT AM I GRATEFUL FOR?




HOW AM I FEELING DURING THIS MOON PHASE?




HOW CAN I IMPROVE MY MINDFULNESS?




WHAT NEW THINGS HAVE I LEARNED ABOUT MYSELF THIS CYCLE?

# LAST QUARTER        NOV 16TH

## MOON IN LEO

This Leo moon will bring out your creative and courageous side. You will feel encouraged to shine and show your unique abilities. This moon is about finding your confidence. Be creative and put yourself out there; share a talent with the world. This is a time for an awakening but make sure to stay grounded while exploring your creativity so that you don't lose your focus.
If you are Leo, you will feel a stronger effect.

## CRYSTALS FOR THIS MOON

Black Obsidian - Cleanses aura, removes negative energy blockages
Lapis Lazuli - Good for self-awareness and revealing inner truth
Clear Quartz - Helps you move toward your deepest desires in life

## MOON AFFIRMATION

I release all blockages that are preventing me from moving forward in abundance. Negative energy will not hold me back.

## MOON RITUAL

Spend time in nature and work on grounding yourself. Take action and release all negative behaviors. Carry your obsidian to protect you from negativity. Burn or carry Geranium oil with you to rebuild your energy after releasing the negativity.

# LAST QUARTER                    NOV 16ᵀᴴ

The Last (Third) Quarter Moon represents a period of release and self-assessment. Cleanse any mental and physical obstacles through organization and meditation.

WHAT HABITS ARE STOPPING ME FROM REACHING MY GOALS?


HOW AM I FEELING DURING THIS MOON PHASE?


WHAT COULD I HAVE DONE DIFFERENTLY DURING THIS CYCLE?


WHAT AM I HOLDING ON TO THAT NEEDS TO BE RELEASED?

# WANING CRESCENT    NOV 17TH–22ND

The Waning Crescent Moon represents a period of surrender and a time for rest.

17TH–18TH IN VIRGO
19TH–21ST IN LIBRA
22ND IN SCORPIO

## CRYSTALS FOR THIS MOON

Bloodstone - helps to embrace the transformation you have been through
Rainbow Fluorite - helps to balance emotions during this up and down period
Black Tourmaline - Grounds your spirit, deflects negative energies
Petalite - Brings peace and calm, supports working with Spirit and angel guides
Black Obsidian - Gently grounding and protective, strengthens your aura field

## MOON AFFIRMATION

I remain centered while my emotions change, and I release any emotions I have been repressing. I can remain balanced and take time to care for myself.

## MOON RITUAL

This moon marks the end of the healing cycle. Think of anything you need to do to complete this cycle before the next one begins. Be gentle to yourself and practice some self-care during this time. Do anything that relaxes you and helps you to feel calm and secure. Take a bath with your crystals surrounding you.

# WANING CRESCENT    NOV 17ᵀᴴ-22ᴺᴰ

HOW CAN I IMPROVE MY SELF-CARE?

HOW AM I FEELING DURING THIS MOON PHASE?

WHAT DO I NEED TO DO FOR MYSELF?

IS THERE ANYTHING IN MY LIFE HOLDING ME BACK?
HOW CAN I LET GO?

# NEW MOON GUIDE  NOV 23ʳᴰ

The Moon will be located on the same side of the Earth as the Sun which means you cannot see the moon from Earth.

## MOON IN SCORPIO

The New Moon in Scorpio offers a new opportunity to look within yourself and healing any darkness in your soul. Focus on letting emotions out and work hard on healing during this time. Face your inner demons and embrace the new life ahead. Now is a good time to pamper yourself by taking a long bath, meditating on your inner power and planting the seeds to your inner desires. If you are a Scorpio, you will feel a stronger effect.

## NEW MOON CRYSTALS

Charge your crystals in this new moon. Leave them out for two nights. You cannot see the moon at this time, but the cleansing is still powerful. Crystals that are powerful in the Scorpio New Moon are: Green Aventurine, Rutilated Quartz and Smoky Quartz. Set your intentions for self-improvement, renewed energy and releasing what you have been holding in your heart.

## NEW MOON RITUAL

Use sage to smudge your space for the ritual. Light a candle. Write down your intentions for the next month on a piece of paper. Meditate on your intentions. In a safe place, light the paper on fire to send your intentions into the universe. Then, take a few moments for yourself. Read a book, take a quiet walk, pray, meditate or rest. Take your crystals to bed with you tonight. You can feel the effects of the moon up to a week before and after it occurs.

# NEW MOON

**NOV 23ʳᴰ**

The New Moon represents a fresh start and new beginnings.

GOALS FOR THIS MOON CYCLE:

HOW AM I FEELING DURING THIS MOON PHASE?

HOW CAN I EXPERIENCE MORE JOY AND PEACE?

WHAT IN MY LIFE NEEDS NOURISHMENT?

# WAXING CRESCENT         NOV 24TH-29TH

The Waxing Crescent Moon Phase represents setting intentions. This moon phase also represents positive changes in your emotional state.

24TH-25TH IN SAGITTARIUS
26TH-27TH IN CAPRICORN
28TH-29TH IN AQUARIUS

## CRYSTALS FOR THIS MOON

Amethyst - brings inspiration, awakens insight and intuition
Citrine - stimulates the brain, promotes motivation and self-expression
Emerald - supports compassion, trust and forgiveness, opens the heart space
Diopside - offers perspective and boosts creativity, great for manifesting visions

## MOON AFFIRMATION

I believe in myself and have confidence in my abilities. My intentions, hopes, and wishes will be reality because I have the power within me to make it happen.

## MOON RITUAL

This moon is in a growth phase and is an exciting time for positive changes in your life. This moon brings growth, luck and love. Carry a Citrine crystal with you to keep you focused and give you confidence to achieve your goals. Review your goals and keep them where you can see them every day.

# WAXING CRESCENT  NOV 24TH-29TH

INTENTIONS FOR THIS MOON CYCLE:

HOW AM I FEELING DURING THIS MOON PHASE?

WHERE DO I FIND INSPIRATION? WHY?

WHAT IS MY BODY FEELING RIGHT NOW?

# FIRST QUARTER          NOV 30TH

## MOON IN PISCES

Pisces is a water sign - the element of great feeling. This moon will bring a higher sense of sensitivity and emotions. You will feel stronger empathy for others and show more compassion for human struggles around you. This moon will also cause you to struggle with concentration and you may find yourself feeling a bit dreamy and lazy. Relax in a long bath, spend time near a large body of water (ocean, lake, etc.), use your imagination on a new project, or help someone in need.

## CRYSTALS FOR THIS MOON

Carnelian - great for motivation, courage and inspiration
Blue Lace Agate - a soothing, calming stone for peace
Lapis Lazuli - helps to open the third eye for heightened intuition

## MOON AFFIRMATION

I am taking action to move toward my dreams by using courage and creativity. I will also remember to take time to care for myself during this cycle.

## MOON RITUAL

Use your Carnelian to create an elixir and sip on it throughout these two days. Place the stone next to a glass of filtered water and leave it by the window to soak up the moon's energy overnight. Say your intentions out loud during this process.

# FIRST QUARTER          NOV 30™

The First Quarter Moon represents a period of growth and action.

ACTION ITEMS FOR THIS MOON CYCLE:

HOW AM I FEELING DURING THIS MOON PHASE?

HOW HAVE I BEEN TAKING ACTION TOWARDS MY GOALS?

ARE MY ACTIONS ALIGNED WITH THE INTENTIONS I HAVE SET FOR MYSELF?

# MONTH-END REFLECTION

WHAT GOALS DID I ACHIEVE THIS PAST MONTH?

WHAT ARE SOME THINGS I CAN IMPROVE ON NEXT MONTH?

WHAT ARE THE THREE MOST IMPORTANT THINGS I LEARNED THIS PAST MONTH?

WHAT DO I LOOK FORWARD TO ACHIEVING NEXT MONTH?

# DECEMBER 2022

1st-6th   WAXING GIBBOUS
7th   FULL MOON
8th-15th   WANING GIBBOUS
16th   LAST QUARTER
17th-22nd   WANING CRESCENT
23rd   NEW MOON
24th-28th   WAXING CRESCENT
29th-30th   FIRST QUARTER
31st   WAXING GIBBOUS

## DECEMBER SOLSTICE
December 21st

(EST USA Time Zone)

# WAXING GIBBOUS         DEC 1ST - 6TH

The Waxing Gibbous Moon represents a period of refining and nurturing your goals, hopes and dreams.

1ST IN PISCES
2ND - 3RD IN ARIES
4TH - 6TH IN TAURUS

## CRYSTALS FOR THIS MOON

Fluorite - activates all Chakras and helps you to find your divine calling
Citrine - attracts success, prosperity and magic; boosts confidence and mental clarity
Pyrite - helps with motivation and taking action toward goals
Tigers Eye - invites good luck, blocks bad luck and negative energies

## MOON AFFIRMATION

I have planted the seeds that will bring me closer to my hopes and dreams. I let positive thoughts grow in my mind and open my heart to all the good things that are coming my way. I see my goals clearly and I feel them manifesting.

## MOON RITUAL

This is the best time to work on yourself and use this amazing healing energy. Push yourself to do more than usual. This is a good time to refine and improve. Carry Pyrite to keep you motivated and take action before the waning phase begins.

# WAXING GIBBOUS     DEC 1ST - 6TH

INTENTIONS I WANT TO NURTURE DURING
THIS MOON CYCLE:

HOW AM I FEELING DURING THIS MOON PHASE?

WHICH GOALS AM I MOST EXCITED ABOUT?

WHAT IS WORKING FOR ME? WHAT IS NOT?
HOW CAN I IMPROVE?

# FULL COLD MOON      DEC 7TH

The Full Moon represents a time to harvest your intentions that have been set and making sure they materialize. The Moon will be located on the opposite side of the Earth as the Sun and its face will be fully illuminated. This full moon was known by early Native American tribes as the Full Cold Moon because this marks the time of year when Winter starts, and the nights are longest.

## MOON IN GEMINI

The Full Cold Moon in Gemini marks a time to be more open and social. You may feel more adventurous during this time and you will be able to easily find fun and humor in everyday occurrences. Be open-minded, try to communicate better and try to be more social during this time. If you are a Gemini, you will feel a stronger effect.

## FULL MOON CRYSTALS

Cleanse your crystals in this full moon. Leave them in the moonlight for two nights to clear any absorbed energies. The best crystals to use for this Gemini Full Moon are: Sodalite, Malachite, Blue Topaz and Que Sera. Clear Quartz is also a very powerful crystal to help balance your Chakras during a Full Moon. Set your intentions to focus on better communication, expressing the truth and trusting your intuition.

## FULL MOON RITUAL

Light a candle, get comfortable and take a few dep breaths. This is best done in the moonlight if possible. Think of a question that you're seeking an answer to. Take a piece of paper and a pen and write your question at the top. Now answer the question freely - letting it flow automatically from within.

# FULL MOON

### DEC 7ᵀᴴ

The Full Moon represents a time to harvest your intentions that have been set and making sure they materialize. You can feel the effects of the moon up to a week before and after it occurs.

**WHAT EMOTIONS AM I FEELING TODAY?**

**WHAT DOES MY SOUL NEED?**

**WHAT HAVE I BEEN NEGLECTING?**

**WHAT AREAS OF MY LIFE FEEL OUT OF ALIGNMENT?**

# WANING GIBBOUS         DEC 8TH-15TH

The Waning Gibbous Moon represents a period of introspection and gratitude. This is also a time to set intentions and declutter your life.

8TH IN GEMINI
9TH-11TH IN CANCER
12TH-13TH IN LEO
14TH-15TH IN VIRGO

## CRYSTALS FOR THIS MOON

Smoky Quartz - Root Chakra, Grounding
Malachite - Cleanse, Purify, Promote positive energy & gratitude
Blue Calcite - Clears negativity and encourages rest & relaxation
Azurite - Strengthens your intuition and psychic abilities
Unakite Jasper - Opens your heart space and brings energy of love

## MOON AFFIRMATION

I am grounded and able to make good decisions. I will be realistic when setting my intentions and goals. I am filled with gratitude for everything that I have.

## MOON RITUAL

Cleanse your home using Palo Santo or Sage. This will make room for positivity in your life and let go of the negativity. Think about anything you need to let go of in your life. Keep a crystal close while you write a list down on paper and create your action plan to let these things go.

# WANING GIBBOUS        DEC 8TH–15TH

WHAT AM I GRATEFUL FOR?




HOW AM I FEELING DURING THIS MOON PHASE?




HOW CAN I IMPROVE MY MINDFULNESS?




WHAT NEW THINGS HAVE I LEARNED ABOUT MYSELF THIS CYCLE?

# LAST QUARTER                      DEC 16TH

## MOON IN VIRGO

Now is a time for decision-making. The strong creative energy inside of you will come to the surface today. Some good activities to do include reading, writing, learning, and teaching. This moon phase will bring the ability to be more productive and accomplish tasks that normally take you longer to complete. This will be a very busy time for you, so make sure to take time to relax as well. Focus on the most important tasks first and remember to stay calm and grounded.
If you are a Virgo, you will feel a stronger effect.

## CRYSTALS FOR THIS MOON

Black Obsidian - Cleanses aura, removes negative energy blockages
Lapis Lazuli - Good for self-awareness and revealing inner truth
Clear Quartz - Helps you move toward your deepest desires in life

## MOON AFFIRMATION

I release all blockages that are preventing me from moving forward in abundance. Negative energy will not hold me back.

## MOON RITUAL

Spend time in nature and work on grounding yourself. Take action and release all negative behaviors. Carry your obsidian to protect you from negativity. Burn or carry Geranium oil with you to rebuild your energy after releasing the negativity.

# LAST QUARTER          DEC 16TH

The Last (Third) Quarter Moon represents a period of release and self-assessment. Cleanse any mental and physical obstacles through organization and meditation.

**WHAT HABITS ARE STOPPING ME FROM REACHING MY GOALS?**

**HOW AM I FEELING DURING THIS MOON PHASE?**

**WHAT COULD I HAVE DONE DIFFERENTLY DURING THIS CYCLE?**

**WHAT AM I HOLDING ON TO THAT NEEDS TO BE RELEASED?**

# WANING CRESCENT          DEC 17TH-22ND

The Waning Crescent Moon represents a period of surrender and a time for rest.

17TH-18TH IN LIBRA
19TH-20TH IN SCORPIO
21ST-22ND IN SAGITTARIUS

## CRYSTALS FOR THIS MOON

Bloodstone - helps to embrace the transformation you have been through
Rainbow Fluorite - helps to balance emotions during this up and down period
Black Tourmaline - Grounds your spirit, deflects negative energies
Petalite - Brings peace and calm, supports working with Spirit and angel guides
Black Obsidian - Gently grounding and protective, strengthens your aura field

## MOON AFFIRMATION

I remain centered while my emotions change, and I release any emotions I have been repressing. I can remain balanced and take time to care for myself.

## MOON RITUAL

This moon marks the end of the healing cycle. Think of anything you need to do to complete this cycle before the next one begins. Be gentle to yourself and practice some self-care during this time. Do anything that relaxes you and helps you to feel calm and secure. Take a bath with your crystals surrounding you.

# WANING CRESCENT    DEC 17TH-22ND

HOW CAN I IMPROVE MY SELF-CARE?

HOW AM I FEELING DURING THIS MOON PHASE?

WHAT DO I NEED TO DO FOR MYSELF?

IS THERE ANYTHING IN MY LIFE HOLDING ME BACK?
HOW CAN I LET GO?

# NEW MOON GUIDE — DEC 23<sup>RD</sup>

The Moon will be located on the same side of the Earth as the Sun which means you cannot see the moon from Earth.

## MOON IN CAPRICORN

The New Moon in Capricorn brings an increased awareness for your need of discipline and structure. This is a good time to work on your budget, being more responsible in certain areas of your life and setting good goals. Now is a time to focus on being stable and patient. This is the best time for planning, organizing, and checking in with yourself to make sure you are on the right path for reaching your goals that you have been setting. If you are a Capricorn, you will feel a stronger effect

## NEW MOON CRYSTALS

Charge your crystals in this new moon. Leave them out for two nights. You cannot see the moon at this time, but the cleansing is still powerful.
Crystals that are powerful in the Capricorn New Moon are: Amethyst, Azurite, Merlinite, Malachite, Clear Quartz, Smoky Quartz, and Tangerine Quartz. Set your intentions for stability and remaining grounded and centered.

## NEW MOON RITUAL

Use sage to smudge your space for the ritual. Light a candle. Write down your intentions for the next month on a piece of paper. Meditate on your intentions. In a safe place, light the paper on fire to send your intentions into the universe. Then, take a few moments for yourself. Read a book, take a quiet walk, pray, meditate or rest. Take your crystals to bed with you tonight. You can feel the effects of the moon up to a week before and after it occurs.

# NEW MOON                           DEC 23ʳᵈ

The New Moon represents a fresh start and new beginnings.

GOALS FOR THIS MOON CYCLE:

HOW AM I FEELING DURING THIS MOON PHASE?

HOW CAN I EXPERIENCE MORE JOY AND PEACE?

WHAT IN MY LIFE NEEDS NOURISHMENT?

# WAXING CRESCENT      DEC 24TH-28TH

The Waxing Crescent Moon Phase represents setting intentions. This moon phase also represents positive changes in your emotional state.

24TH IN CAPRICORN
25TH-26TH IN AQUARIUS
27TH-28TH IN PISCES

## CRYSTALS FOR THIS MOON

Amethyst - brings inspiration, awakens insight and intuition
Citrine - stimulates the brain, promotes motivation and self-expression
Emerald - supports compassion, trust and forgiveness, opens the heart space
Diopside - offers perspective and boosts creativity, great for manifesting visions

## MOON AFFIRMATION

I believe in myself and have confidence in my abilities. My intentions, hopes, and wishes will be reality because I have the power within me to make it happen.

## MOON RITUAL

This moon is in a growth phase and is an exciting time for positive changes in your life. This moon brings growth, luck and love. Carry a Citrine crystal with you to keep you focused and give you confidence to achieve your goals. Review your goals and keep them where you can see them every day.

# WAXING CRESCENT  DEC 24TH-28TH

INTENTIONS FOR THIS MOON CYCLE:

HOW AM I FEELING DURING THIS MOON PHASE?

WHERE DO I FIND INSPIRATION? WHY?

WHAT IS MY BODY FEELING RIGHT NOW?

# FIRST QUARTER            DEC 29TH–30TH

## MOON IN ARIES

The moon in Aries can cause you to feel more impulsive, direct and powerful. When combined with the First Quarter moon, you will start taking action. This moon will spark your desires and passions. You will feel a burst of momentum to attack your goals headfirst! Take advantage of this time for great change.

## CRYSTALS FOR THIS MOON

Carnelian - great for motivation, courage and inspiration
Blue Lace Agate - a soothing, calming stone for peace
Lapis Lazuli - helps to open the third eye for heightened intuition

## MOON AFFIRMATION

I am taking action to move toward my dreams by using courage and creativity. I will also remember to take time to care for myself during this cycle.

## MOON RITUAL

Use your Carnelian to create an elixir and sip on it throughout these two days. Place the stone next to a glass of filtered water and leave it by the window to soak up the moon's energy overnight. Say your intentions out loud during this process.

# FIRST QUARTER  DEC 29TH-30TH

The First Quarter Moon represents a period of growth and action.

ACTION ITEMS FOR THIS MOON CYCLE:




HOW AM I FEELING DURING THIS MOON PHASE?




HOW HAVE I BEEN TAKING ACTION TOWARDS
MY GOALS?




ARE MY ACTIONS ALIGNED WITH THE INTENTIONS
I HAVE SET FOR MYSELF?

# WAXING GIBBOUS　　　　　DEC 31ˢᵀ

The Waxing Gibbous Moon represents a period of refining and nurturing your goals, hopes and dreams.

## IN ARIES

## CRYSTALS FOR THIS MOON

Fluorite - activates all Chakras and helps you to find your divine calling
Citrine - attracts success, prosperity and magic; boosts confidence and mental clarity
Pyrite - helps with motivation and taking action toward goals
Tigers Eye - invites good luck, blocks bad luck and negative energies

## MOON AFFIRMATION

I have planted the seeds that will bring me closer to my hopes and dreams. I let positive thoughts grow in my mind and open my heart to all the good things that are coming my way. I see my goals clearly and I feel them manifesting.

## MOON RITUAL

This is the best time to work on yourself and use this amazing healing energy. Push yourself to do more than usual. This is a good time to refine and improve. Carry Pyrite to keep you motivated and take action before the waning phase begins.

# WAXING GIBBOUS          DEC 31ST

INTENTIONS I WANT TO NURTURE DURING
THIS MOON CYCLE:

HOW AM I FEELING DURING THIS MOON PHASE?

WHICH GOALS AM I MOST EXCITED ABOUT?

WHAT IS WORKING FOR ME? WHAT IS NOT?
HOW CAN I IMPROVE?

# END OF YEAR REFLECTION

WHAT DID I ACCOMPLISH THIS YEAR THAT I AM MOST PROUD OF?

WHAT WOULD I DO DIFFERENTLY NEXT YEAR?

WHAT DID I LEARN ABOUT MYSELF THIS YEAR?

WHAT DO I LOOK FORWARD TO ACHIEVING NEXT YEAR?

# THANK YOU!

I am beyond grateful that you chose to purchase my book from thousands of options. I hope this moon journal has allowed you a safe space for healing and processing your thoughts. I also hope that you continue your healing journey by purchasing your new moon journal for next year. If you are interested in learning more about other journals, please check out my Amazon author page "Mystic Tortoise" by using the link below. I also create beautiful gifts and healing crystal jewelry in my Etsy shop - please check it out as well.

I wish you all the very best in the future!


Link to all of my Pages using Link Tree:
https://linktr.ee/Mystictortoise

Made in the USA
Middletown, DE
17 December 2021